C-679   CAREER EXAMINATION SERIES

*This is your
PASSBOOK for...*

Recreation Director

*Test Preparation Study Guide
Questions & Answers*

NATIONAL LEARNING CORPORATION®

COPYRIGHT NOTICE

This book is SOLELY intended for, is sold ONLY to, and its use is RESTRICTED to individual, bona fide applicants or candidates who qualify by virtue of having seriously filed applications for appropriate license, certificate, professional and/or promotional advancement, higher school matriculation, scholarship, or other legitimate requirements of education and/or governmental authorities.

This book is NOT intended for use, class instruction, tutoring, training, duplication, copying, reprinting, excerption, or adaptation, etc., by:

1) Other publishers
2) Proprietors and/or Instructors of "Coaching" and/or Preparatory Courses
3) Personnel and/or Training Divisions of commercial, industrial, and governmental organizations
4) Schools, colleges, or universities and/or their departments and staffs, including teachers and other personnel
5) Testing Agencies or Bureaus
6) Study groups which seek by the purchase of a single volume to copy and/or duplicate and/or adapt this material for use by the group as a whole without having purchased individual volumes for each of the members of the group
7) Et al.

Such persons would be in violation of appropriate Federal and State statutes.

PROVISION OF LICENSING AGREEMENTS – Recognized educational, commercial, industrial, and governmental institutions and organizations, and others legitimately engaged in educational pursuits, including training, testing, and measurement activities, may address request for a licensing agreement to the copyright owners, who will determine whether, and under what conditions, including fees and charges, the materials in this book may be used them. In other words, a licensing facility exists for the legitimate use of the material in this book on other than an individual basis. However, it is asseverated and affirmed here that the material in this book CANNOT be used without the receipt of the express permission of such a licensing agreement from the Publishers. Inquiries re licensing should be addressed to the company, attention rights and permissions department.

All rights reserved, including the right of reproduction in whole or in part, in any form or by any means, electronic or mechanical, including photocopying, recording, or by any information storage and retrieval system, without permission in writing from the Publisher.

Copyright © 2024 by
National Learning Corporation

212 Michael Drive, Syosset, NY 11791
(516) 921-8888 • www.passbooks.com
E-mail: info@passbooks.com

PUBLISHED IN THE UNITED STATES OF AMERICA

PASSBOOK® SERIES

THE *PASSBOOK® SERIES* has been created to prepare applicants and candidates for the ultimate academic battlefield – the examination room.

At some time in our lives, each and every one of us may be required to take an examination – for validation, matriculation, admission, qualification, registration, certification, or licensure.

Based on the assumption that every applicant or candidate has met the basic formal educational standards, has taken the required number of courses, and read the necessary texts, the *PASSBOOK® SERIES* furnishes the one special preparation which may assure passing with confidence, instead of failing with insecurity. Examination questions – together with answers – are furnished as the basic vehicle for study so that the mysteries of the examination and its compounding difficulties may be eliminated or diminished by a sure method.

This book is meant to help you pass your examination provided that you qualify and are serious in your objective.

The entire field is reviewed through the huge store of content information which is succinctly presented through a provocative and challenging approach – the question-and-answer method.

A climate of success is established by furnishing the correct answers at the end of each test.

You soon learn to recognize types of questions, forms of questions, and patterns of questioning. You may even begin to anticipate expected outcomes.

You perceive that many questions are repeated or adapted so that you can gain acute insights, which may enable you to score many sure points.

You learn how to confront new questions, or types of questions, and to attack them confidently and work out the correct answers.

You note objectives and emphases, and recognize pitfalls and dangers, so that you may make positive educational adjustments.

Moreover, you are kept fully informed in relation to new concepts, methods, practices, and directions in the field.

You discover that you are actually taking the examination all the time: you are preparing for the examination by "taking" an examination, not by reading extraneous and/or supererogatory textbooks.

In short, this PASSBOOK®, used directedly, should be an important factor in helping you to pass your test.

RECREATION DIRECTOR

DUTIES
The work involves administration and implementation of a comprehensive community recreation program. An employee in this class has responsibility for developing, coordinating and implementing sports and recreation programs. The incumbent directs a staff responsible for supervising day-to-day operations of the division. Work is performed under the general direction of the department head and is reviewed through conferences and reports. Does related work as required.

SCOPE OF THE EXAMINATION
The written test will cover knowledge, skills and abilities in such areas as:

1. Recreation administration;
2. Principles and practices of leisure recreation;
3. Supervision;
4. Educating and interacting with the public; and
5. Preparing written material.

HOW TO TAKE A TEST

I. YOU MUST PASS AN EXAMINATION

A. WHAT EVERY CANDIDATE SHOULD KNOW

Examination applicants often ask us for help in preparing for the written test. What can I study in advance? What kinds of questions will be asked? How will the test be given? How will the papers be graded?

As an applicant for a civil service examination, you may be wondering about some of these things. Our purpose here is to suggest effective methods of advance study and to describe civil service examinations.

Your chances for success on this examination can be increased if you know how to prepare. Those "pre-examination jitters" can be reduced if you know what to expect. You can even experience an adventure in good citizenship if you know why civil service exams are given.

B. WHY ARE CIVIL SERVICE EXAMINATIONS GIVEN?

Civil service examinations are important to you in two ways. As a citizen, you want public jobs filled by employees who know how to do their work. As a job seeker, you want a fair chance to compete for that job on an equal footing with other candidates. The best-known means of accomplishing this two-fold goal is the competitive examination.

Exams are widely publicized throughout the nation. They may be administered for jobs in federal, state, city, municipal, town or village governments or agencies.

Any citizen may apply, with some limitations, such as the age or residence of applicants. Your experience and education may be reviewed to see whether you meet the requirements for the particular examination. When these requirements exist, they are reasonable and applied consistently to all applicants. Thus, a competitive examination may cause you some uneasiness now, but it is your privilege and safeguard.

C. HOW ARE CIVIL SERVICE EXAMS DEVELOPED?

Examinations are carefully written by trained technicians who are specialists in the field known as "psychological measurement," in consultation with recognized authorities in the field of work that the test will cover. These experts recommend the subject matter areas or skills to be tested; only those knowledges or skills important to your success on the job are included. The most reliable books and source materials available are used as references. Together, the experts and technicians judge the difficulty level of the questions.

Test technicians know how to phrase questions so that the problem is clearly stated. Their ethics do not permit "trick" or "catch" questions. Questions may have been tried out on sample groups, or subjected to statistical analysis, to determine their usefulness.

Written tests are often used in combination with performance tests, ratings of training and experience, and oral interviews. All of these measures combine to form the best-known means of finding the right person for the right job.

II. HOW TO PASS THE WRITTEN TEST

A. NATURE OF THE EXAMINATION

To prepare intelligently for civil service examinations, you should know how they differ from school examinations you have taken. In school you were assigned certain definite pages to read or subjects to cover. The examination questions were quite detailed and usually emphasized memory. Civil service exams, on the other hand, try to discover your present ability to perform the duties of a position, plus your potentiality to learn these duties. In other words, a civil service exam attempts to predict how successful you will be. Questions cover such a broad area that they cannot be as minute and detailed as school exam questions.

In the public service similar kinds of work, or positions, are grouped together in one "class." This process is known as *position-classification*. All the positions in a class are paid according to the salary range for that class. One class title covers all of these positions, and they are all tested by the same examination.

B. FOUR BASIC STEPS

1) Study the announcement

How, then, can you know what subjects to study? Our best answer is: "Learn as much as possible about the class of positions for which you've applied." The exam will test the knowledge, skills and abilities needed to do the work.

Your most valuable source of information about the position you want is the official exam announcement. This announcement lists the training and experience qualifications. Check these standards and apply only if you come reasonably close to meeting them.

The brief description of the position in the examination announcement offers some clues to the subjects which will be tested. Think about the job itself. Review the duties in your mind. Can you perform them, or are there some in which you are rusty? Fill in the blank spots in your preparation.

Many jurisdictions preview the written test in the exam announcement by including a section called "Knowledge and Abilities Required," "Scope of the Examination," or some similar heading. Here you will find out specifically what fields will be tested.

2) Review your own background

Once you learn in general what the position is all about, and what you need to know to do the work, ask yourself which subjects you already know fairly well and which need improvement. You may wonder whether to concentrate on improving your strong areas or on building some background in your fields of weakness. When the announcement has specified "some knowledge" or "considerable knowledge," or has used adjectives like "beginning principles of…" or "advanced … methods," you can get a clue as to the number and difficulty of questions to be asked in any given field. More questions, and hence broader coverage, would be included for those subjects which are more important in the work. Now weigh your strengths and weaknesses against the job requirements and prepare accordingly.

3) Determine the level of the position

Another way to tell how intensively you should prepare is to understand the level of the job for which you are applying. Is it the entering level? In other words, is this the position in which beginners in a field of work are hired? Or is it an intermediate or advanced level? Sometimes this is indicated by such words as "Junior" or "Senior" in the class title. Other jurisdictions use Roman numerals to designate the level – Clerk I, Clerk II, for example. The word "Supervisor" sometimes appears in the title. If the level is not indicated by the title, check the description of duties. Will you be working under very close supervision, or will you have responsibility for independent decisions in this work?

4) Choose appropriate study materials

Now that you know the subjects to be examined and the relative amount of each subject to be covered, you can choose suitable study materials. For beginning level jobs, or even advanced ones, if you have a pronounced weakness in some aspect of your training, read a modern, standard textbook in that field. Be sure it is up to date and has general coverage. Such books are normally available at your library, and the librarian will be glad to help you locate one. For entry-level positions, questions of appropriate difficulty are chosen — neither highly advanced questions, nor those too simple. Such questions require careful thought but not advanced training.

If the position for which you are applying is technical or advanced, you will read more advanced, specialized material. If you are already familiar with the basic principles of your field, elementary textbooks would waste your time. Concentrate on advanced textbooks and technical periodicals. Think through the concepts and review difficult problems in your field.

These are all general sources. You can get more ideas on your own initiative, following these leads. For example, training manuals and publications of the government agency which employs workers in your field can be useful, particularly for technical and professional positions. A letter or visit to the government department involved may result in more specific study suggestions, and certainly will provide you with a more definite idea of the exact nature of the position you are seeking.

III. KINDS OF TESTS

Tests are used for purposes other than measuring knowledge and ability to perform specified duties. For some positions, it is equally important to test ability to make adjustments to new situations or to profit from training. In others, basic mental abilities not dependent on information are essential. Questions which test these things may not appear as pertinent to the duties of the position as those which test for knowledge and information. Yet they are often highly important parts of a fair examination. For very general questions, it is almost impossible to help you direct your study efforts. What we can do is to point out some of the more common of these general abilities needed in public service positions and describe some typical questions.

1) General information

Broad, general information has been found useful for predicting job success in some kinds of work. This is tested in a variety of ways, from vocabulary lists to questions about current events. Basic background in some field of work, such as sociology or economics, may be sampled in a group of questions. Often these are principles which have become familiar to most persons through exposure rather than through formal training. It is difficult to advise you how to study for these questions; being alert to the world around you is our best suggestion.

2) Verbal ability

An example of an ability needed in many positions is verbal or language ability. Verbal ability is, in brief, the ability to use and understand words. Vocabulary and grammar tests are typical measures of this ability. Reading comprehension or paragraph interpretation questions are common in many kinds of civil service tests. You are given a paragraph of written material and asked to find its central meaning.

3) Numerical ability
Number skills can be tested by the familiar arithmetic problem, by checking paired lists of numbers to see which are alike and which are different, or by interpreting charts and graphs. In the latter test, a graph may be printed in the test booklet which you are asked to use as the basis for answering questions.

4) Observation
A popular test for law-enforcement positions is the observation test. A picture is shown to you for several minutes, then taken away. Questions about the picture test your ability to observe both details and larger elements.

5) Following directions
In many positions in the public service, the employee must be able to carry out written instructions dependably and accurately. You may be given a chart with several columns, each column listing a variety of information. The questions require you to carry out directions involving the information given in the chart.

6) Skills and aptitudes
Performance tests effectively measure some manual skills and aptitudes. When the skill is one in which you are trained, such as typing or shorthand, you can practice. These tests are often very much like those given in business school or high school courses. For many of the other skills and aptitudes, however, no short-time preparation can be made. Skills and abilities natural to you or that you have developed throughout your lifetime are being tested.

Many of the general questions just described provide all the data needed to answer the questions and ask you to use your reasoning ability to find the answers. Your best preparation for these tests, as well as for tests of facts and ideas, is to be at your physical and mental best. You, no doubt, have your own methods of getting into an exam-taking mood and keeping "in shape." The next section lists some ideas on this subject.

IV. KINDS OF QUESTIONS

Only rarely is the "essay" question, which you answer in narrative form, used in civil service tests. Civil service tests are usually of the short-answer type. Full instructions for answering these questions will be given to you at the examination. But in case this is your first experience with short-answer questions and separate answer sheets, here is what you need to know:

1) Multiple-choice Questions
Most popular of the short-answer questions is the "multiple choice" or "best answer" question. It can be used, for example, to test for factual knowledge, ability to solve problems or judgment in meeting situations found at work.
A multiple-choice question is normally one of three types—
- It can begin with an incomplete statement followed by several possible endings. You are to find the one ending which *best* completes the statement, although some of the others may not be entirely wrong.
- It can also be a complete statement in the form of a question which is answered by choosing one of the statements listed.

- It can be in the form of a problem – again you select the best answer.

Here is an example of a multiple-choice question with a discussion which should give you some clues as to the method for choosing the right answer:

When an employee has a complaint about his assignment, the action which will *best* help him overcome his difficulty is to
- A. discuss his difficulty with his coworkers
- B. take the problem to the head of the organization
- C. take the problem to the person who gave him the assignment
- D. say nothing to anyone about his complaint

In answering this question, you should study each of the choices to find which is best. Consider choice "A" – Certainly an employee may discuss his complaint with fellow employees, but no change or improvement can result, and the complaint remains unresolved. Choice "B" is a poor choice since the head of the organization probably does not know what assignment you have been given, and taking your problem to him is known as "going over the head" of the supervisor. The supervisor, or person who made the assignment, is the person who can clarify it or correct any injustice. Choice "C" is, therefore, correct. To say nothing, as in choice "D," is unwise. Supervisors have and interest in knowing the problems employees are facing, and the employee is seeking a solution to his problem.

2) True/False Questions

The "true/false" or "right/wrong" form of question is sometimes used. Here a complete statement is given. Your job is to decide whether the statement is right or wrong.

SAMPLE: A roaming cell-phone call to a nearby city costs less than a non-roaming call to a distant city.

This statement is wrong, or false, since roaming calls are more expensive.

This is not a complete list of all possible question forms, although most of the others are variations of these common types. You will always get complete directions for answering questions. Be sure you understand *how* to mark your answers – ask questions until you do.

V. RECORDING YOUR ANSWERS

Computer terminals are used more and more today for many different kinds of exams.
For an examination with very few applicants, you may be told to record your answers in the test booklet itself. Separate answer sheets are much more common. If this separate answer sheet is to be scored by machine – and this is often the case – it is highly important that you mark your answers correctly in order to get credit.
An electronic scoring machine is often used in civil service offices because of the speed with which papers can be scored. Machine-scored answer sheets must be marked with a pencil, which will be given to you. This pencil has a high graphite content which responds to the electronic scoring machine. As a matter of fact, stray dots may register as answers, so do not let your pencil rest on the answer sheet while you are pondering the correct answer. Also, if your pencil lead breaks or is otherwise defective, ask for another.

Since the answer sheet will be dropped in a slot in the scoring machine, be careful not to bend the corners or get the paper crumpled.

The answer sheet normally has five vertical columns of numbers, with 30 numbers to a column. These numbers correspond to the question numbers in your test booklet. After each number, going across the page are four or five pairs of dotted lines. These short dotted lines have small letters or numbers above them. The first two pairs may also have a "T" or "F" above the letters. This indicates that the first two pairs only are to be used if the questions are of the true-false type. If the questions are multiple choice, disregard the "T" and "F" and pay attention only to the small letters or numbers.

Answer your questions in the manner of the sample that follows:

32. The largest city in the United States is
    A. Washington, D.C.
    B. New York City
    C. Chicago
    D. Detroit
    E. San Francisco

1) Choose the answer you think is best. (New York City is the largest, so "B" is correct.)
2) Find the row of dotted lines numbered the same as the question you are answering. (Find row number 32)
3) Find the pair of dotted lines corresponding to the answer. (Find the pair of lines under the mark "B.")
4) Make a solid black mark between the dotted lines.

VI. BEFORE THE TEST

Common sense will help you find procedures to follow to get ready for an examination. Too many of us, however, overlook these sensible measures. Indeed, nervousness and fatigue have been found to be the most serious reasons why applicants fail to do their best on civil service tests. Here is a list of reminders:

- Begin your preparation early – Don't wait until the last minute to go scurrying around for books and materials or to find out what the position is all about.
- Prepare continuously – An hour a night for a week is better than an all-night cram session. This has been definitely established. What is more, a night a week for a month will return better dividends than crowding your study into a shorter period of time.
- Locate the place of the exam – You have been sent a notice telling you when and where to report for the examination. If the location is in a different town or otherwise unfamiliar to you, it would be well to inquire the best route and learn something about the building.
- Relax the night before the test – Allow your mind to rest. Do not study at all that night. Plan some mild recreation or diversion; then go to bed early and get a good night's sleep.
- Get up early enough to make a leisurely trip to the place for the test – This way unforeseen events, traffic snarls, unfamiliar buildings, etc. will not upset you.
- Dress comfortably – A written test is not a fashion show. You will be known by number and not by name, so wear something comfortable.

- Leave excess paraphernalia at home – Shopping bags and odd bundles will get in your way. You need bring only the items mentioned in the official notice you received; usually everything you need is provided. Do not bring reference books to the exam. They will only confuse those last minutes and be taken away from you when in the test room.
- Arrive somewhat ahead of time – If because of transportation schedules you must get there very early, bring a newspaper or magazine to take your mind off yourself while waiting.
- Locate the examination room – When you have found the proper room, you will be directed to the seat or part of the room where you will sit. Sometimes you are given a sheet of instructions to read while you are waiting. Do not fill out any forms until you are told to do so; just read them and be prepared.
- Relax and prepare to listen to the instructions
- If you have any physical problem that may keep you from doing your best, be sure to tell the test administrator. If you are sick or in poor health, you really cannot do your best on the exam. You can come back and take the test some other time.

VII. AT THE TEST

The day of the test is here and you have the test booklet in your hand. The temptation to get going is very strong. Caution! There is more to success than knowing the right answers. You must know how to identify your papers and understand variations in the type of short-answer question used in this particular examination. Follow these suggestions for maximum results from your efforts:

1) Cooperate with the monitor

The test administrator has a duty to create a situation in which you can be as much at ease as possible. He will give instructions, tell you when to begin, check to see that you are marking your answer sheet correctly, and so on. He is not there to guard you, although he will see that your competitors do not take unfair advantage. He wants to help you do your best.

2) Listen to all instructions

Don't jump the gun! Wait until you understand all directions. In most civil service tests you get more time than you need to answer the questions. So don't be in a hurry. Read each word of instructions until you clearly understand the meaning. Study the examples, listen to all announcements and follow directions. Ask questions if you do not understand what to do.

3) Identify your papers

Civil service exams are usually identified by number only. You will be assigned a number; you must not put your name on your test papers. Be sure to copy your number correctly. Since more than one exam may be given, copy your exact examination title.

4) Plan your time

Unless you are told that a test is a "speed" or "rate of work" test, speed itself is usually not important. Time enough to answer all the questions will be provided, but this does not mean that you have all day. An overall time limit has been set. Divide the total time (in minutes) by the number of questions to determine the approximate time you have for each question.

5) Do not linger over difficult questions

If you come across a difficult question, mark it with a paper clip (useful to have along) and come back to it when you have been through the booklet. One caution if you do this – be sure to skip a number on your answer sheet as well. Check often to be sure that you have not lost your place and that you are marking in the row numbered the same as the question you are answering.

6) Read the questions

Be sure you know what the question asks! Many capable people are unsuccessful because they failed to *read* the questions correctly.

7) Answer all questions

Unless you have been instructed that a penalty will be deducted for incorrect answers, it is better to guess than to omit a question.

8) Speed tests

It is often better NOT to guess on speed tests. It has been found that on timed tests people are tempted to spend the last few seconds before time is called in marking answers at random – without even reading them – in the hope of picking up a few extra points. To discourage this practice, the instructions may warn you that your score will be "corrected" for guessing. That is, a penalty will be applied. The incorrect answers will be deducted from the correct ones, or some other penalty formula will be used.

9) Review your answers

If you finish before time is called, go back to the questions you guessed or omitted to give them further thought. Review other answers if you have time.

10) Return your test materials

If you are ready to leave before others have finished or time is called, take ALL your materials to the monitor and leave quietly. Never take any test material with you. The monitor can discover whose papers are not complete, and taking a test booklet may be grounds for disqualification.

VIII. EXAMINATION TECHNIQUES

1) Read the general instructions carefully. These are usually printed on the first page of the exam booklet. As a rule, these instructions refer to the timing of the examination; the fact that you should not start work until the signal and must stop work at a signal, etc. If there are any *special* instructions, such as a choice of questions to be answered, make sure that you note this instruction carefully.

2) When you are ready to start work on the examination, that is as soon as the signal has been given, read the instructions to each question booklet, underline any key words or phrases, such as *least, best, outline, describe* and the like. In this way you will tend to answer as requested rather than discover on reviewing your paper that you *listed without describing*, that you selected the *worst* choice rather than the *best* choice, etc.

3) If the examination is of the objective or multiple-choice type – that is, each question will also give a series of possible answers: A, B, C or D, and you are called upon to select the best answer and write the letter next to that answer on your answer paper – it is advisable to start answering each question in turn. There may be anywhere from 50 to 100 such questions in the three or four hours allotted and you can see how much time would be taken if you read through all the questions before beginning to answer any. Furthermore, if you come across a question or group of questions which you know would be difficult to answer, it would undoubtedly affect your handling of all the other questions.

4) If the examination is of the essay type and contains but a few questions, it is a moot point as to whether you should read all the questions before starting to answer any one. Of course, if you are given a choice – say five out of seven and the like – then it is essential to read all the questions so you can eliminate the two that are most difficult. If, however, you are asked to answer all the questions, there may be danger in trying to answer the easiest one first because you may find that you will spend too much time on it. The best technique is to answer the first question, then proceed to the second, etc.

5) Time your answers. Before the exam begins, write down the time it started, then add the time allowed for the examination and write down the time it must be completed, then divide the time available somewhat as follows:
    - If 3-1/2 hours are allowed, that would be 210 minutes. If you have 80 objective-type questions, that would be an average of 2-1/2 minutes per question. Allow yourself no more than 2 minutes per question, or a total of 160 minutes, which will permit about 50 minutes to review.
    - If for the time allotment of 210 minutes there are 7 essay questions to answer, that would average about 30 minutes a question. Give yourself only 25 minutes per question so that you have about 35 minutes to review.

6) The most important instruction is to *read each question* and make sure you know what is wanted. The second most important instruction is to *time yourself properly* so that you answer every question. The third most important instruction is to *answer every question*. Guess if you have to but include something for each question. Remember that you will receive no credit for a blank and will probably receive some credit if you write something in answer to an essay question. If you guess a letter – say "B" for a multiple-choice question – you may have guessed right. If you leave a blank as an answer to a multiple-choice question, the examiners may respect your feelings but it will not add a point to your score. Some exams may penalize you for wrong answers, so in such cases *only*, you may not want to guess unless you have some basis for your answer.

7) Suggestions
    a. Objective-type questions
        1. Examine the question booklet for proper sequence of pages and questions
        2. Read all instructions carefully
        3. Skip any question which seems too difficult; return to it after all other questions have been answered
        4. Apportion your time properly; do not spend too much time on any single question or group of questions

5. Note and underline key words – *all, most, fewest, least, best, worst, same, opposite,* etc.
6. Pay particular attention to negatives
7. Note unusual option, e.g., unduly long, short, complex, different or similar in content to the body of the question
8. Observe the use of "hedging" words – *probably, may, most likely,* etc.
9. Make sure that your answer is put next to the same number as the question
10. Do not second-guess unless you have good reason to believe the second answer is definitely more correct
11. Cross out original answer if you decide another answer is more accurate; do not erase until you are ready to hand your paper in
12. Answer all questions; guess unless instructed otherwise
13. Leave time for review

   b. Essay questions
   1. Read each question carefully
   2. Determine exactly what is wanted. Underline key words or phrases.
   3. Decide on outline or paragraph answer
   4. Include many different points and elements unless asked to develop any one or two points or elements
   5. Show impartiality by giving pros and cons unless directed to select one side only
   6. Make and write down any assumptions you find necessary to answer the questions
   7. Watch your English, grammar, punctuation and choice of words
   8. Time your answers; don't crowd material

8) Answering the essay question

Most essay questions can be answered by framing the specific response around several key words or ideas. Here are a few such key words or ideas:

M's: manpower, materials, methods, money, management
P's: purpose, program, policy, plan, procedure, practice, problems, pitfalls, personnel, public relations

   a. Six basic steps in handling problems:
   1. Preliminary plan and background development
   2. Collect information, data and facts
   3. Analyze and interpret information, data and facts
   4. Analyze and develop solutions as well as make recommendations
   5. Prepare report and sell recommendations
   6. Install recommendations and follow up effectiveness

   b. Pitfalls to avoid
   1. *Taking things for granted* – A statement of the situation does not necessarily imply that each of the elements is necessarily true; for example, a complaint may be invalid and biased so that all that can be taken for granted is that a complaint has been registered

2. *Considering only one side of a situation* – Wherever possible, indicate several alternatives and then point out the reasons you selected the best one
3. *Failing to indicate follow up* – Whenever your answer indicates action on your part, make certain that you will take proper follow-up action to see how successful your recommendations, procedures or actions turn out to be
4. *Taking too long in answering any single question* – Remember to time your answers properly

IX. AFTER THE TEST

Scoring procedures differ in detail among civil service jurisdictions although the general principles are the same. Whether the papers are hand-scored or graded by machine we have described, they are nearly always graded by number. That is, the person who marks the paper knows only the number – never the name – of the applicant. Not until all the papers have been graded will they be matched with names. If other tests, such as training and experience or oral interview ratings have been given, scores will be combined. Different parts of the examination usually have different weights. For example, the written test might count 60 percent of the final grade, and a rating of training and experience 40 percent. In many jurisdictions, veterans will have a certain number of points added to their grades.

After the final grade has been determined, the names are placed in grade order and an eligible list is established. There are various methods for resolving ties between those who get the same final grade – probably the most common is to place first the name of the person whose application was received first. Job offers are made from the eligible list in the order the names appear on it. You will be notified of your grade and your rank as soon as all these computations have been made. This will be done as rapidly as possible.

People who are found to meet the requirements in the announcement are called "eligibles." Their names are put on a list of eligible candidates. An eligible's chances of getting a job depend on how high he stands on this list and how fast agencies are filling jobs from the list.

When a job is to be filled from a list of eligibles, the agency asks for the names of people on the list of eligibles for that job. When the civil service commission receives this request, it sends to the agency the names of the three people highest on this list. Or, if the job to be filled has specialized requirements, the office sends the agency the names of the top three persons who meet these requirements from the general list.

The appointing officer makes a choice from among the three people whose names were sent to him. If the selected person accepts the appointment, the names of the others are put back on the list to be considered for future openings.

That is the rule in hiring from all kinds of eligible lists, whether they are for typist, carpenter, chemist, or something else. For every vacancy, the appointing officer has his choice of any one of the top three eligibles on the list. This explains why the person whose name is on top of the list sometimes does not get an appointment when some of the persons lower on the list do. If the appointing officer chooses the second or third eligible, the No. 1 eligible does not get a job at once, but stays on the list until he is appointed or the list is terminated.

X. HOW TO PASS THE INTERVIEW TEST

The examination for which you applied requires an oral interview test. You have already taken the written test and you are now being called for the interview test – the final part of the formal examination.

You may think that it is not possible to prepare for an interview test and that there are no procedures to follow during an interview. Our purpose is to point out some things you can do in advance that will help you and some good rules to follow and pitfalls to avoid while you are being interviewed.

What is an interview supposed to test?

The written examination is designed to test the technical knowledge and competence of the candidate; the oral is designed to evaluate intangible qualities, not readily measured otherwise, and to establish a list showing the relative fitness of each candidate – as measured against his competitors – for the position sought. Scoring is not on the basis of "right" and "wrong," but on a sliding scale of values ranging from "not passable" to "outstanding." As a matter of fact, it is possible to achieve a relatively low score without a single "incorrect" answer because of evident weakness in the qualities being measured.

Occasionally, an examination may consist entirely of an oral test – either an individual or a group oral. In such cases, information is sought concerning the technical knowledges and abilities of the candidate, since there has been no written examination for this purpose. More commonly, however, an oral test is used to supplement a written examination.

Who conducts interviews?

The composition of oral boards varies among different jurisdictions. In nearly all, a representative of the personnel department serves as chairman. One of the members of the board may be a representative of the department in which the candidate would work. In some cases, "outside experts" are used, and, frequently, a businessman or some other representative of the general public is asked to serve. Labor and management or other special groups may be represented. The aim is to secure the services of experts in the appropriate field.

However the board is composed, it is a good idea (and not at all improper or unethical) to ascertain in advance of the interview who the members are and what groups they represent. When you are introduced to them, you will have some idea of their backgrounds and interests, and at least you will not stutter and stammer over their names.

What should be done before the interview?

While knowledge about the board members is useful and takes some of the surprise element out of the interview, there is other preparation which is more substantive. It *is* possible to prepare for an oral interview – in several ways:

1) Keep a copy of your application and review it carefully before the interview

This may be the only document before the oral board, and the starting point of the interview. Know what education and experience you have listed there, and the sequence and dates of all of it. Sometimes the board will ask you to review the highlights of your experience for them; you should not have to hem and haw doing it.

2) Study the class specification and the examination announcement

Usually, the oral board has one or both of these to guide them. The qualities, characteristics or knowledges required by the position sought are stated in these documents. They offer valuable clues as to the nature of the oral interview. For example, if the job involves supervisory responsibilities, the announcement will usually indicate that knowledge of modern supervisory methods and the qualifications of the candidate as a supervisor will be tested. If so, you can expect such questions, frequently in the form of a hypothetical situation which you are expected to solve. NEVER go into an oral without knowledge of the duties and responsibilities of the job you seek.

3) Think through each qualification required

Try to visualize the kind of questions you would ask if you were a board member. How well could you answer them? Try especially to appraise your own knowledge and background in each area, *measured against the job sought*, and identify any areas in which you are weak. Be critical and realistic – do not flatter yourself.

4) Do some general reading in areas in which you feel you may be weak

For example, if the job involves supervision and your past experience has NOT, some general reading in supervisory methods and practices, particularly in the field of human relations, might be useful. Do NOT study agency procedures or detailed manuals. The oral board will be testing your understanding and capacity, not your memory.

5) Get a good night's sleep and watch your general health and mental attitude

You will want a clear head at the interview. Take care of a cold or any other minor ailment, and of course, no hangovers.

What should be done on the day of the interview?

Now comes the day of the interview itself. Give yourself plenty of time to get there. Plan to arrive somewhat ahead of the scheduled time, particularly if your appointment is in the fore part of the day. If a previous candidate fails to appear, the board might be ready for you a bit early. By early afternoon an oral board is almost invariably behind schedule if there are many candidates, and you may have to wait. Take along a book or magazine to read, or your application to review, but leave any extraneous material in the waiting room when you go in for your interview. In any event, relax and compose yourself.

The matter of dress is important. The board is forming impressions about you – from your experience, your manners, your attitude, and your appearance. Give your personal appearance careful attention. Dress your best, but not your flashiest. Choose conservative, appropriate clothing, and be sure it is immaculate. This is a business interview, and your appearance should indicate that you regard it as such. Besides, being well groomed and properly dressed will help boost your confidence.

Sooner or later, someone will call your name and escort you into the interview room. *This is it.* From here on you are on your own. It is too late for any more preparation. But remember, you asked for this opportunity to prove your fitness, and you are here because your request was granted.

What happens when you go in?

The usual sequence of events will be as follows: The clerk (who is often the board stenographer) will introduce you to the chairman of the oral board, who will introduce you to the other members of the board. Acknowledge the introductions before you sit down. Do not be surprised if you find a microphone facing you or a stenotypist sitting by. Oral interviews are usually recorded in the event of an appeal or other review.

Usually the chairman of the board will open the interview by reviewing the highlights of your education and work experience from your application – primarily for the benefit of the other members of the board, as well as to get the material into the record. Do not interrupt or comment unless there is an error or significant misinterpretation; if that is the case, do not hesitate. But do not quibble about insignificant matters. Also, he will usually ask you some question about your education, experience or your present job – partly to get you to start talking and to establish the interviewing "rapport." He may start the actual questioning, or turn it over to one of the other members. Frequently, each member undertakes the questioning on a particular area, one in which he is perhaps most competent, so you can expect each member to participate in the examination. Because time is limited, you may also expect some rather abrupt switches in the direction the questioning takes, so do not be upset by it. Normally, a board member will not pursue a single line of questioning unless he discovers a particular strength or weakness.

After each member has participated, the chairman will usually ask whether any member has any further questions, then will ask you if you have anything you wish to add. Unless you are expecting this question, it may floor you. Worse, it may start you off on an extended, extemporaneous speech. The board is not usually seeking more information. The question is principally to offer you a last opportunity to present further qualifications or to indicate that you have nothing to add. So, if you feel that a significant qualification or characteristic has been overlooked, it is proper to point it out in a sentence or so. Do not compliment the board on the thoroughness of their examination – they have been sketchy, and you know it. If you wish, merely say, "No thank you, I have nothing further to add." This is a point where you can "talk yourself out" of a good impression or fail to present an important bit of information. Remember, *you close the interview yourself.*

The chairman will then say, "That is all, Mr. _____, thank you." Do not be startled; the interview is over, and quicker than you think. Thank him, gather your belongings and take your leave. Save your sigh of relief for the other side of the door.

How to put your best foot forward

Throughout this entire process, you may feel that the board individually and collectively is trying to pierce your defenses, seek out your hidden weaknesses and embarrass and confuse you. Actually, this is not true. They are obliged to make an appraisal of your qualifications for the job you are seeking, and they want to see you in your best light. Remember, they must interview all candidates and a non-cooperative candidate may become a failure in spite of their best efforts to bring out his qualifications. Here are 15 suggestions that will help you:

1) Be natural – Keep your attitude confident, not cocky

If you are not confident that you can do the job, do not expect the board to be. Do not apologize for your weaknesses, try to bring out your strong points. The board is interested in a positive, not negative, presentation. Cockiness will antagonize any board member and make him wonder if you are covering up a weakness by a false show of strength.

2) Get comfortable, but don't lounge or sprawl

Sit erectly but not stiffly. A careless posture may lead the board to conclude that you are careless in other things, or at least that you are not impressed by the importance of the occasion. Either conclusion is natural, even if incorrect. Do not fuss with your clothing, a pencil or an ashtray. Your hands may occasionally be useful to emphasize a point; do not let them become a point of distraction.

3) Do not wisecrack or make small talk

This is a serious situation, and your attitude should show that you consider it as such. Further, the time of the board is limited – they do not want to waste it, and neither should you.

4) Do not exaggerate your experience or abilities

In the first place, from information in the application or other interviews and sources, the board may know more about you than you think. Secondly, you probably will not get away with it. An experienced board is rather adept at spotting such a situation, so do not take the chance.

5) If you know a board member, do not make a point of it, yet do not hide it

Certainly you are not fooling him, and probably not the other members of the board. Do not try to take advantage of your acquaintanceship – it will probably do you little good.

6) Do not dominate the interview

Let the board do that. They will give you the clues – do not assume that you have to do all the talking. Realize that the board has a number of questions to ask you, and do not try to take up all the interview time by showing off your extensive knowledge of the answer to the first one.

7) Be attentive

You only have 20 minutes or so, and you should keep your attention at its sharpest throughout. When a member is addressing a problem or question to you, give him your undivided attention. Address your reply principally to him, but do not exclude the other board members.

8) Do not interrupt

A board member may be stating a problem for you to analyze. He will ask you a question when the time comes. Let him state the problem, and wait for the question.

9) Make sure you understand the question

Do not try to answer until you are sure what the question is. If it is not clear, restate it in your own words or ask the board member to clarify it for you. However, do not haggle about minor elements.

10) Reply promptly but not hastily

A common entry on oral board rating sheets is "candidate responded readily," or "candidate hesitated in replies." Respond as promptly and quickly as you can, but do not jump to a hasty, ill-considered answer.

11) Do not be peremptory in your answers

A brief answer is proper – but do not fire your answer back. That is a losing game from your point of view. The board member can probably ask questions much faster than you can answer them.

12) Do not try to create the answer you think the board member wants

He is interested in what kind of mind you have and how it works – not in playing games. Furthermore, he can usually spot this practice and will actually grade you down on it.

13) Do not switch sides in your reply merely to agree with a board member

Frequently, a member will take a contrary position merely to draw you out and to see if you are willing and able to defend your point of view. Do not start a debate, yet do not surrender a good position. If a position is worth taking, it is worth defending.

14) Do not be afraid to admit an error in judgment if you are shown to be wrong

The board knows that you are forced to reply without any opportunity for careful consideration. Your answer may be demonstrably wrong. If so, admit it and get on with the interview.

15) Do not dwell at length on your present job

The opening question may relate to your present assignment. Answer the question but do not go into an extended discussion. You are being examined for a *new* job, not your present one. As a matter of fact, try to phrase ALL your answers in terms of the job for which you are being examined.

Basis of Rating

Probably you will forget most of these "do's" and "don'ts" when you walk into the oral interview room. Even remembering them all will not ensure you a passing grade. Perhaps you did not have the qualifications in the first place. But remembering them will help you to put your best foot forward, without treading on the toes of the board members.

Rumor and popular opinion to the contrary notwithstanding, an oral board wants you to make the best appearance possible. They know you are under pressure – but they also want to see how you respond to it as a guide to what your reaction would be under the pressures of the job you seek. They will be influenced by the degree of poise you display, the personal traits you show and the manner in which you respond.

ABOUT THIS BOOK

This book contains tests divided into Examination Sections. Go through each test, answering every question in the margin. We have also attached a sample answer sheet at the back of the book that can be removed and used. At the end of each test look at the answer key and check your answers. On the ones you got wrong, look at the right answer choice and learn. Do not fill in the answers first. Do not memorize the questions and answers, but understand the answer and principles involved. On your test, the questions will likely be different from the samples. Questions are changed and new ones added. If you understand these past questions you should have success with any changes that arise. Tests may consist of several types of questions. We have additional books on each subject should more study be advisable or necessary for you. Finally, the more you study, the better prepared you will be. This book is intended to be the last thing you study before you walk into the examination room. Prior study of relevant texts is also recommended. NLC publishes some of these in our Fundamental Series. Knowledge and good sense are important factors in passing your exam. Good luck also helps. So now study this Passbook, absorb the material contained within and take that knowledge into the examination. Then do your best to pass that exam.

EXAMINATION SECTION

EXAMINATION SECTION
TEST 1

DIRECTIONS: Each question or incomplete statement is followed by several suggested answers or completions. Select the one that BEST answers the question or completes the statement. *PRINT THE LETTER OF THE CORRECT ANSWER IN THE SPACE AT THE RIGHT.*

1. The _____ goals of a park and recreation department consist of those outcomes the agency seeks to achieve by offering programs. 1._____

    A. external
    B. adaptation
    C. positional
    D. management

2. Most recreation professionals would include each of the following in a definition of *recreation* EXCEPT 2._____

    A. requiring personal and free choice on the part of the recreationist
    B. requiring a commitment by the recreationist
    C. rewarding insofar as the recreationist can establish and meet certain specific goals
    D. occurring during nonobligated time

3. For what type of bond is a *sinkable* fund generally used? 3._____

    A. Callable
    B. Serial
    C. Assessment
    D. Term

4. Which of the following would be involved in an assessment of a manager's socioemotional skills? 4._____

    A. Efficiency orientation
    B. Self-control
    C. Conceptualization
    D. Logical thought

5. Which of the following is NOT a typical guideline to be used in community recreation programming? 5._____

    A. Community recreation should meet significant social needs.
    B. Special groups in the community, such as the mentally or physically disabled, should be served by recreation programs that meet their social, emotional, creative, and physical needs.
    C. Recreational activities should involve fixed schedules, locations, and personnel that community members will be able to rely upon and schedule around with few surprises.
    D. Community recreation programs should be meaningfully interpreted to the public at large through effective public relations media and community relations activities.

6. The maintenance department of a park and recreation agency should maintain a workload file containing all copies of submitted forms. Which of the following is NOT a convincing reason for this? 6._____

    A. Workers often forget their assignments.
    B. The completed tasks reveal a dollar value useful during budgeting.

C. Originals may get lost.
D. A special request for priority consideration be made if delays jeopardize safety or morale.

7. As part of an overall effort to reduce costs, park and recreation departments are likely to decrease expenditures related to budget items such as each of the following EXCEPT

   A. gasoline consumption and number of vehicles in department pools
   B. purchase of consumable supplies (paper, paint, crayons, basketballs, etc.) that are dispensed to the public without fee or accountability
   C. special programs that are seasonal or infrequently scheduled
   D. subscriptions, memberships, and purchase of books and training films

8. The National Recreation and Park Association recommends that if a public swimming pool is built for a community, it provide _____ square feet of swimming area of every 1% to 3% of the community population.

   A. 5   B. 15   C. 25   D. 40

9. According to surveys of park and recreation employees at the non-managerial level, the MOST important motivating factor for working in the field is

   A. being part of a team and not letting them down
   B. good working conditions
   C. doing work that is perceived by the employee to be important and worthwhile
   D. appreciation by supervisors for work performed

10. In programming recreational sports contests or tournaments, a department sometimes declines to take complete responsibility for scheduling, and relies instead on a system of *instant* scheduling. Each of the following is an advantage associated with this system EXCEPT

    A. it encourages entries well before the final deadline
    B. participants do not need to be contacted until playoff time, unless there is a schedule change
    C. there is no need for a large physical setting to conduct the process for large numbers of people
    D. selection of alternate playing times is done by participants

11. The _____ budget represents a combination of the object and function classification methods.

    A. performance
    B. classification by fund
    C. classification by organizational units
    D. operating

12. In budget planning sessions, a diagraph can be used to provide information about each of the following EXCEPT

    A. areas of needed program service
    B. months of greatest and least congestion
    C. geographical relations between major facilities
    D. conflicts among special events

13. A summer camp program includes rigidly planned meals, a rising hour, and bedtime, but other phases of the program are planned by both counselors and campers. This program could best be described as

    A. totally nonstructured
    B. having a skeletal structure
    C. semistructured
    D. fully structured

14. Typically, policymaking in public agencies is determined by each of the following EXCEPT

    A. departmental factors
    B. recommendations of professional societies
    C. recommendations of clientele
    D. professional literature

15. Which of the following is considered to be the responsibility of a program staff member at a park and recreation department?

    A. Attending to equipment
    B. Supervising a playground
    C. Monitoring the operating budget
    D. Helping plan policies and procedures

16. It is generally NOT a purpose of a public park and recreation department's public relations efforts to

    A. attempt to coordinate the actions and attitudes of the public and the organization that seeks to serve it
    B. disseminate information to the public
    C. alter the public's beliefs and actions through persuasion
    D. parry the negative efforts of political foes within the municipality or region

17. In deciding whether or not to engage in a certain recreational activity, which of the following steps would a person typically assess FIRST?

    A. His or her own personal suitability to the activity
    B. The probability that participation actually will result in possible benefits
    C. The relative value of the activity
    D. The feasibility of participating

18. A public park and recreation agency's most commonly exercised method of acquiring property for facilities is to

    A. secure an easement
    B. transfer lands or exchange properties from one government department to another
    C. compel subdividers into setting aside property for recreational and park use
    D. purchase the property directly from its owner

19. In most litigation involving park and recreation departments, which of the following is LEAST likely to be the target of litigious action?

    A. The program sponsor
    B. Administrators or supervisors
    C. The employee whose conduct is a direct or proximate cause of the injury
    D. A volunteer serving as an administrative adviser

20. After recreation programs have been initially planned and presented, each of the following concepts will be useful to consider in making program modifications EXCEPT

    A. required facilities
    B. program life cycle
    C. methods of program presentation
    D. program structure and degree of centralization

21. With which of the following statements, about the unionization of park and recreation workers, would an agency head most likely DISAGREE? It has

    A. improved the welfare of the employees by gaining for them higher salaries and benefits than they would have otherwise received
    B. enhanced the organization's ability to offer programs and services on the days and at the times when they are most desired by the public
    C. enhanced management's ability to hire well-qualified personnel
    D. forced the organization to reduce the quantity of services it provides for the public

22. Which of the following is NOT likely to be included in the land records of a park and recreation department?

    A. Where the official deeds are filed
    B. Official actions affecting the title such as street vacations, etc.
    C. Non-liability insurance records
    D. Legal description of the land

23. A manager responds to an employee's grievance by saying he feels sorry for the employee, but cannot do anything to change the situation. The manager has offered a(n) _____ response.

    A. situational   B. sympathetic
    C. judgmental   D. empathetic

24. In a working environment involving a mature group, the leader defines what is to be done, but engages also in supporting behavior intended to contribute to the group's willingness to work at a task. According to situational leadership theory, this mode of leadership is called

    A. participating   B. telling
    C. selling   D. delegating

25. For a large organization such as a park and recreation department, the MOST important aspect of maintaining financial controls is/are
    A. keeping adequate financial records and preparing and submitting monthly reports relating expenditures to categories in the annual budget
    B. establishing and enforcing strict cost control procedures
    C. the department's procedures for purchasing supplies or equipment
    D. the department's procedural requirements for making and enforcing contractual agreements

KEY (CORRECT ANSWERS)

1. A
2. C
3. D
4. B
5. C

6. A
7. C
8. B
9. C
10. C

11. A
12. C
13. B
14. C
15. C

16. D
17. C
18. D
19. D
20. A

21. B
22. C
23. B
24. C
25. A

TEST 2

DIRECTIONS: Each question or incomplete statement is followed by several suggested answers or completions. Select the one that BEST answers the question or completes the statement. *PRINT THE LETTER OF THE CORRECT ANSWER IN THE SPACE AT THE RIGHT.*

1. Each of the following is a type of supervisory board or commission associated with public recreation and park departments EXCEPT 1.____

    A. semi-independent bodies with the power to make policy, but dependent on a higher governmental body that provides funding and to which they must report
    B. advisory boards or commissions with limited powers
    C. completely independent bodies with full authority for establishing and overseeing policy
    D. independent bodies which do not make policy, but are primarily responsible for locating and distributing funds associated with policies formulated by another body

2. Which of the following is NOT a key managerial function in the process of organizing? 2.____

    A. Determination of recruitment and hiring policies
    B. Defining goals and objectives
    C. Clustering functions within the organization
    D. Assigning responsibility to individuals and granting authority

3. The authority for raising taxes and spending money for municipal recreation services comes from 3.____

    A. state legislatures
    B. the local board
    C. local elections
    D. the welfare clauses of the Constitution

4. Studies in public parks and recreation departments have shown that although the public shows initial resistance to the imposition of new or increased fees for use of programs, services, and facilities, the short-term decline in usage tends to disappear within 4.____

    A. 6-8 months   B. 12-18 months
    C. 2-3 years   D. 3-5 years

5. For legal purposes, the standard of care owed to a user by a park and recreation department is determined by classifying the types of users into three broad categories. Which of the following is NOT one of these categories? 5.____

    A. Licensee   B. Trespasser
    C. Invitee   D. Grantee

6. The primary *disadvantage* associated with the use of a double-elimination format for scheduled recreational tournaments is that 6.____

    A. it does not tend to hold the interest of participants
    B. the format is often confusing for participants to follow
    C. it is perceived as being unfair
    D. it does not allow a participant to have an *off day*

7. When estimating the short-term recreational facility demand projections for a community, a manager should describe the agency's actions to be taken over the next _____ years.

    A. 1-2   B. 3-5   C. 5-10   D. 15

7.____

8. If the existence of an *attractive nuisance* can be proved, a park and recreation department can be found liable for an injury to a person who has illegally trespassed onto an unsupervised facility.
Each of the following conditions is necessary in order to prove the existence of an *attractive nuisance* EXCEPT

    A. the trespasser is a child who is judged to be too young to know better
    B. the property is not completely enclosed by a fence at least 6 feet in height
    C. the agency or owner of the land upon which the child trespasses is aware that the area is attractive to children
    D. a dangerous condition exists on the property that is not a natural hazard

8.____

9. Within a working group, the degree to which a situation is favorable or unfavorable for the use of a task-oriented leadership style is MOST dependent on

    A. the quality of leader-member relationships
    B. task structure
    C. the size of the group
    D. the leader's position power

9.____

10. A park and recreation department leases a golf course to another agency. In terms of liability, the department is practicing risk

    A. avoidance   B. reduction
    C. transfer   D. retention

10.____

11. Cost accounting is useful to a park and recreation department in each of the following ways EXCEPT

    A. determining the proper balance between different phases of departmental operation
    B. evaluating individual personnel performance
    C. evaluating expenditures referenced to different elements of the community population
    D. determining the feasibility of constructing facilities with either the agency's own labor or on a contractual basis

11.____

12. The contract method of scheduling personnel in a park and recreation department is unrealistic when

    A. positions require specialization
    B. personnel qualifications and availability are consistent
    C. employees wish to select their own days and shifts
    D. the system requires the establishment of work schedules for a specific time span

12.____

13. In the personnel classification system traditionally used in public agencies such as park and recreation departments, supervisors are normally responsible for

    A. coordinating and directing the overall work of the department
    B. overseeing responsibilities within a geographical area or district of a community

13.____

C. planning, organizing, and directly supervising recreation programs in one or more facilities
D. recruiting, selecting, assigning, and supervising all department personnel

14. Which of the following steps in a municipal park planning procedure is generally performed FIRST?

    A. The preliminary design
    B. Inspection of the site with topographic map in hand
    C. The making of the investigative report
    D. Working drawings and specifications

15. When a manager or supervisor relies upon a(n) _____ style of leadership, the reaction of employees will most often be hostility and aggression within members of the group.

    A. laissez-faire   B. democratic
    C. authoritative   D. autocratic

16. Which of the following approaches to recreation program development is focused on the need to provide programs that are responsive to community pressures and influences?

    A. Traditional   B. Expressed desires
    C. Sociopolitical   D. Current practices

17. Risk retention is a valid policy for a park and recreation department under each of the following conditions EXCEPT when

    A. the maximum possible loss is so small that the agency can absorb it in the operating budget
    B. it is possible to transfer the risks to another
    C. the probability of a loss is so low that it can be ignored
    D. the cost to transfer the risk is so high that it would cost almost as much as the worst loss that could occur

18. Most public park and recreation department contracts with other organizations fall into several clearly defined categories. Which of the following is LEAST likely to be one of these?

    A. Direct programming and leadership of department services
    B. The purchase of equipment, materials, and supplies
    C. Planning, design, or construction of capital facilities
    D. Arrangements for concessions, franchises, or leases of special types of service or facilities

19. To make an agency's services more effective, supervision of staff should be thought of as a(n) _____ process.

    A. permissive   B. directing
    C. enabling   D. controlling

20. Which type of commercial leisure-service organizations account for the greatest dollar-volume of annual sales?

    A. Partnerships   B. Institutions
    C. Corporations   D. Sole proprietorships

21. In addition to public resistance to the implementation of a fee structure for certain services or facilities, a park and recreation department may encounter some administrative problems. Which of the following is NOT typically one of these problems?   21.____

    A. The fees may be illegal in some cases
    B. Difficulty in controlling access to services where fees are levied
    C. The exclusion of certain disadvantaged groups may present an unmanageable apparatus
    D. The cost of administering fees may be more than the revenues generated by it

22. When composing a grant proposal, which of the following pieces of information will probably be LEAST useful to the reader?   22.____

    A. Demonstration of critical need
    B. Capital facilities that can be used as collateral
    C. A precise statement of the budget
    D. Availability of matching funds

23. To be most effective in his or her leadership role, a manager in a park and recreation department should be each of the following EXCEPT   23.____

    A. optimistic   B. aggressive
    C. resilient   D. reactive

24. Recreation and park administrators should involve themselves as fully as possible in each construction project — according to each of the following guidelines EXCEPT   24.____

    A. become familiar with all background information related to the facility plan and be actively involved in all public hearings
    B. be present at the first design conference to make sure program needs are considered, and then obtaining a summary of each modification session
    C. insist that all construction details or standards be carried out exactly as specified
    D. visit the construction site regularly, once construction begins, either with staff members or with the architect

25. Volunteers at a park and recreation department are LEAST likely to assist in   25.____

    A. the budgeting process
    B. program delivery
    C. logistical services
    D. an administrative-advisory capacity

KEY (CORRECT ANSWERS)

1. D
2. A
3. D
4. C
5. D

6. B
7. B
8. B
9. A
10. C

11. C
12. A
13. B
14. C
15. D

16. C
17. B
18. A
19. C
20. C

21. C
22. B
23. D
24. B
25. A

EXAMINATION SECTION
TEST 1

DIRECTIONS: Each question or incomplete statement is followed by several suggested answers or completions. Select the one that BEST answers the question or completes the statement. *PRINT THE LETTER OF THE CORRECT ANSWER IN THE SPACE AT THE RIGHT.*

1. For a large public park and recreation department, it is generally agreed that the key to productivity is

    A. contracting and leasing arrangements
    B. the effective management of personnel
    C. cost-benefit analysis
    D. appealing to private foundations for funds

    1._____

2. In a park and recreation setting, four conditions must be present in a situation in order for the department to be found legally negligent, and therefore liable, in the case of an accident. Which of the following is NOT one of these conditions?

    A. Proof of injury or damage
    B. Legal responsibility for the participant
    C. The participant's lack of an employment relationship to the department
    D. The department's failure to take reasonable care

    2._____

3. In a park and recreation department, the MOST effective approach to problem-solving is generally described as

    A. group-centered
    B. authoritarian
    C. decisions by higher authorities
    D. an analysis by planning specialists

    3._____

4. Which of the following administration philosophies or strategies is part of the future-oriented trend in park and recreation management?

    A. Planning programs with the staff, chiefly by updating past programs
    B. Evaluating outcomes primarily through attendance figures
    C. Providing programs and services based on social and economic needs of the community
    D. Requiring financial accountability and justifying budgets based on historical precedent

    4._____

5. The _____ approach to leisure service sees recreation as an important community service that is carried on both for its own sake and because it contributes to the mental and physical health of participants.

    A. human-services   B. prescriptive
    C. environmental   D. quality-of-life

    5._____

6. More or increased _____ is NOT a growing trend in leisure services.

    A. centralized personnel structure
    B. emphasis on health and fitness

    6._____

11

C. consideration of leisure's contribution to quality of life
D. emphasis on noncompetitive forms of play

7. The MOST common means of financing public recreation and park departments is through

   A. bonds
   B. grants
   C. taxes
   D. fees and charges

8. For evaluating the effectiveness of specific programs offered by a park and recreation department, each of the following methods is commonly used EXCEPT

   A. systems-based, goal-achievement models
   B. internal auditing by top management
   C. staff-based evaluation processes
   D. participant-based evaluation

9. A public agency that favors the delegation of authority is BEST described as

   A. heterogeneous
   B. decentralized
   C. individualistic
   D. irresponsible

10. The ability to _____ is NOT generally considered to be a core process that an entry-level employee in a park and recreation department should master.

    A. carry out both program planning and organizational planning
    B. formally articulate resource needs
    C. utilize leadership processes
    D. teach

11. A _____ budget is designed in such a way that large units of work, or special programs, are isolated, identified, and described in detail.

    A. object classification
    B. function classification
    C. program
    D. performance

12. When programming recreational activities for participants in middle childhood (6-12 years), it is important to remember that they are generally

    A. preferring separation into sexually segregated groups
    B. physically aggressive
    C. physically growing more quickly than in preschool years
    D. unconcerned about ideas such as competence, achievement, and approval from others

13. Of the following issues, _____ is LEAST likely to be negotiated in a park and recreation labor union contractual agreement.

    A. work hours
    B. contracting work, or *outsourcing*
    C. safety regulations
    D. retirement plans

14. Which of the following is considered to be the responsibility of an auxiliary staff member at a park and recreation department?   14._____

    A. Supervision of sport programs
    B. Monitoring adherence to agency rules
    C. Direction of administrative guidelines
    D. Organizing sport activities

15. Traditionally, leisure facilities have been planned according to   15._____

    A. concepts of the neighborhood and community
    B. urban planning methods based on land-use principles
    C. a needs index
    D. recommended standards of open space

16. Public agencies such as park and recreation departments typically use one of several contemporary models in evaluating whether the agency has achieved its stated objectives. Which of the following is NOT one of these models?
Evaluation designed to measure the   16._____

    A. overall quality of programs, based on the opinion of an advisory board
    B. effectiveness of programs in meeting their stated goals and objectives
    C. effectiveness of personnel in carrying out stated program goals and objectives
    D. level of satisfaction of program participants

17. It is NOT typically a function of a public park and recreation agency's board or commission to   17._____

    A. review and approve all policies and work with the agency's managers to develop plans for meeting present and future leisure needs of the community
    B. consider and approve all personnel appointments or promotions
    C. articulate to the agency's director and staff how the details of administration should be carried out
    D. carry out long-range planning in cooperation with other community organizations to meet public recreational needs

18. In handling employment inquiries, application forms, and interviews for employment, questions to the applicant about _____ may be allowed under law, whether their use is job-related or not.   18._____

    A. employment history
    B. physical requirements
    C. arrest and conviction record
    D. age

19. According to most current practices in public agencies, any overspending or underspending in the year's budget is to be brought to the department head's attention in the month of   19._____

    A. January   B. February
    C. March or April   D. November

20. In order to avoid legal liability for certain activities involving children, some park and recreation departments use the convention of permission slips signed by a parent or guardian, in which they are asked to waive the right to sue in case of injury or accident. For several reasons, these slips offer the department a false sense of security. Which of the following is NOT one of these reasons?
    I. In all cases, signed statements are invalid if the risks of the activity are not understood.
    II. The waiver is not valid unless signed by both parents, no matter what their geographic location.
    III. They cannot waive the right of a child to bring suit against the agency when the child reaches the legal age for doing so.

    The CORRECT answer is:

    A. I only   B. I, II   C. I, III   D. I, II, III

21. Which of the following recreation facilities would most likely be located at or near the intersection of major or secondary thoroughfares near the center of a 4- or 5-square mile service area?

    A. Playlot
    B. Large park
    C. Playground
    D. Athletic field

22. Which of the following is NOT a level of planning commonly associated with recreation and park facilities?

    A. Planning that focuses solely on recreation and park development within a total community, sometimes as a separate portion of a total plan
    B. Regional planning that takes into account services and facilities offered by adjacent jurisdictions
    C. Planning that is concerned with the development of a particular facility or the needs of a single neighborhood
    D. Total master planning that considers all aspects of municipal growth, including industrial and residential development, transportation, education, housing, health, etc.

23. The MAIN advantage of a structured, centralized approach to recreational programming is

    A. being able to respond to local neighborhood needs
    B. optimum legal protection from liability claims
    C. more efficient use of personnel resources
    D. a set of clear-cut standards for fulfilling the agency's stated objectives

24. When programming recreational activities for participants in middle adulthood (40-65 years), it is important to remember that they generally

    A. experience physiological changes in the brain
    B. begin to experience instability in cognitive skills
    C. display a loss of creativity
    D. tend to gain weight easily

25. In park and recreation accounting, concurrent auditing represents 25.____
    A. a preaudit of expected income or disbursements
    B. a formal check of specific administrative or program divisions of a department, or construction or maintenance projects
    C. a form of bookkeeping report showing the assets and liabilities of a given fund or budget
    D. all departmental expenditures that have been authorized and carried out

KEY (CORRECT ANSWERS)

1.	B		11.	C
2.	C		12.	A
3.	A		13.	B
4.	C		14.	A
5.	D		15.	C
6.	A		16.	A
7.	C		17.	C
8.	B		18.	A
9.	B		19.	B
10.	B		20.	C

21. D
22. B
23. D
24. D
25. A

TEST 2

DIRECTIONS: Each question or incomplete statement is followed by several suggested answers or completions. Select the one that BEST answers the question or completes the statement. *PRINT THE LETTER OF THE CORRECT ANSWER IN THE SPACE AT THE RIGHT.*

1. Each of the following is a benefit associated with the use of a *matrix* structure in a public park and recreation department EXCEPT

    A. greater opportunity of employees' personal development
    B. better technical performance
    C. improved flexibility in conditions of change and uncertainty
    D. involvement in long-range planning of employees at every level

    1._____

2. Which of the following statements about recreationists in early adulthood (20-39 years) is generally TRUE?

    A. They are more self-centered than adolescents.
    B. Their friendships are characterized by less intimacy.
    C. They experience a lack of stability in intellectual skills.
    D. They expand their social relationships through new contacts within the occupational and community settings.

    2._____

3. When programming recreation activities, an administrator's choices are likely to be affected by each of the following factors EXCEPT

    A. the number of potential activities
    B. the characteristics of participants
    C. the funds required
    D. personnel

    3._____

4. A recreation programmer wants to stage a single-elimination summer softball tournament at the department's facilities. Each of the following is an advantage associated with the single-elimination format EXCEPT it

    A. is usually more interesting for spectators
    B. may accommodate a large number of participants
    C. encourages maximum participation
    D. is the most economical to conduct

    4._____

5. In a recreation or park facility's off-season, an administrator wants to maintain a minimum level of care. Typically, how often should litter at the facility be picked up?

    A. Daily   B. Weekly
    C. Monthly   D. Every two months

    5._____

6. Funding agencies for public park and recreation departments have historically applied strict criteria for determining grant recipients. Which of the following statements about their considerations is generally FALSE?

    A. There must be evidence that existing programs and facilities are being fully utilized.
    B. Agencies applying for grants must be prepared to guarantee a substantial portion of the total grant proposal.

    6._____

C. Higher priority is given to proposals that come from more than one agency or sponsor.
D. Wherever possible, grant proposals should be designed to serve the general population, rather than isolated or special-need communities.

7. In public recreation programs, sport accounts for about _____% of all active involvement.

    A. 10-30　　　B. 35-50　　　C. 60-75　　　D. 80-95

8. Which of the following is NOT a level of responsibility defined by the functional classification of personnel analysis?

    A. Managerial　　　B. Tutorial
    C. Logistical　　　D. Operational

9. During a community needs assessment, a park and recreation department would most likely conduct use surveys among the community members in order to determine the _____ leisure needs of the community.

    A. expressed　　　B. normative　　　C. relative　　　D. perceived

10. The main disadvantage to using an *object classification* type of budget for a park and recreation department is that

    A. it does not relate expenditures meaningfully to programs
    B. certain expenditures, such as personnel, are not considered *objects*
    C. it does not provide complete itemization of expenditures
    D. it does not take unplanned expenditures into account

11. Which of the following is NOT a guideline to follow in preparing a newspaper release for a public park and recreation department event or service?

    A. The release should stick to the facts and avoid editorializing.
    B. An attempt should be made to feature a prominent or interesting individual or group of people in the article.
    C. The most important information should be included at the beginning of the article.
    D. The release should be limited to 2 or 3 pages.

12. In a public school or college's recreational facilities, the priority of use must be

    A. intramural or campus recreational programming
    B. intercollegiate practice sessions or competition
    C. formal academic program use
    D. community residents

13. For a supervisor in a park and recreation department, each of the following is a guideline to follow in taking disciplinary action with employees EXCEPT

    A. when correction is required, it should be handled in private
    B. the worker should be told what he or she can do to correct the situation
    C. the action should not be taken until some time after the need for it has been established
    D. take the same corrective actions for the same behaviors with different individuals

14. The healthiest way a park and recreation department manager can approach the subject   14.____
    of inter-employee conflict is to view it as

    A. inevitable, but desirable and able to be used to constructive ends
    B. a healthy sign that workers in the department intend to challenge and compete
       with one another to meet departmental goals
    C. an inevitable product of a close working relationship that should be not denied, but
       endured peaceably
    D. a harmful and destructive influence that should be avoided at all costs

15. Which of the following is NOT generally considered to be a guideline to follow in deter-   15.____
    mining when, and for what, recreation fees and charges are justified?

    A. Frequently charge where *preservation* is the dominant function
    B. Be sure that some benefit accrues to the taxpayer
    C. The specific services to be charged for and the fee should be matters of local
       choice
    D. Frequently charge where *use* is the dominant function

16. Generally, which of the following approaches to urban planning is used LEAST often?   16.____

    A. Developing an ideal model of the community
    B. Cost-revenue model
    C. User-oriented approach
    D. Needs index model

17. When conditions within a working group are only moderately favorable or unfavorable   17.____
    (i.e., the leader is well-liked but the task under consideration is unstructured),
    what type of leadership style is most appropriate?

    A. Laissez-faire   B. Task-oriented
    C. Authoritarian   D. Relationship-oriented

18. In a park and recreation department, a cost-benefit analysis is LEAST likely to be useful   18.____
    for

    A. identifying high- and low-cost programs and services as related to maintenance,
       administration, and direct leadership costs per participant-hour of service rendered
    B. providing valuable support data for justifying budget requests
    C. providing essential data for determining the cost-effectiveness of individual depart-
       ment personnel
    D. permitting the assignment of priorities to specific programs and services

19. In recent years, the number of volunteers working for public park and recreation depart-   19.____
    ments has increased among certain segments of the population. Among the following
    groups, which has shown the LEAST significant increase in volunteer service?

    A. Females   B. Males
    C. Poor people   D. Minorities

20. The major type of legislation affecting parks and recreation is the   20.____

    A. regulatory law   B. special district law
    C. enabling law   D. home rule legislation

21. When programming recreational activities for participants in late adulthood (over 65 years), it is important to remember that they generally

    A. do not require a significant restructuring of time
    B. have a self-concept that tends to be more dependent upon external factors
    C. prefer to live in close contact with others of their age group
    D. become less active if they are men, and more active if they are women

22. The self-study approach to agency evaluation, outlined by the National Recreation and Park Association, includes standards that are used in measuring the effectiveness of a department in several major categories. Which of the following is NOT one of these categories?

    A. Administration
    B. Evaluation
    C. Programming
    D. Funding

23. Decisions made at the lower level of an agency's management, which are part of operational planning and program implementation, are described as _____ decisions.

    A. primary
    B. problem-oriented
    C. reflex
    D. task-oriented

24. In park and recreation applications, a *flowchart* is used to

    A. view the community-wide availability of programs and detect under- or over-provision of different types of activities on a geographical basis
    B. show all events or continuing activities in a convenient and easily understood form
    C. show individual projects or programs laid out along a calendar, with specific tasks indicated for the dates on which they are to be begun and completed
    D. identify major facilities and ongoing programs

25. In recreation and sports injury cases involving parents and children, the parents, but not the child, can be barred from recovery for a child's injury under certain conditions. Which of the following is NOT one of these conditions?
    The

    A. parent has failed to exercise reasonable care to prevent the child from placing himself in a situation in which lack of self-protective capacity may reasonably be expected to result in harm to the child
    B. child is too young to exercise self-protection
    C. child's incapacity is a contributing factor in harm
    D. injury involves an *attractive nuisance*

KEY (CORRECT ANSWERS)

1. D
2. D
3. A
4. C
5. A

6. D
7. C
8. B
9. D
10. A

11. D
12. C
13. C
14. A
15. A

16. B
17. D
18. C
19. A
20. C

21. D
22. D
23. D
24. C
25. D

EXAMINATION SECTION
TEST 1

DIRECTIONS: Each question or incomplete statement is followed by several suggested answers or completions. Select the one that BEST answers the question or completes the statement. *PRINT THE LETTER OF THE CORRECT ANSWER IN THE SPACE AT THE RIGHT.*

1. A well-conceived and effectively presented budget should do each of the following EXCEPT

    A. inform taxpayers and government officials of the amounts of money spent, the sources of revenue, and the costs of achieving departmental goals
    B. serve for evaluating the program and ensuring that objectives are met
    C. help in promoting flexible operational procedures by creating very few classifications for all expenditures, and requiring flexible procedures for approving them
    D. provide a general statement of the financial needs, resources, and plans of the department, including an outline of all program elements and their costs and allocations for facilities and personnel

    1.____

2. Among volunteers who offer time to park and recreation departments, which of the following motivating factors is most prevalent?

    A. Preparation for paid employment
    B. Family influences
    C. A desire to feel needed
    D. A desire to be helpful

    2.____

3. Which of the following approaches to leisure service is found chiefly among recreation and park managers who serve in resource-based agencies?

    A. Individualist
    B. Prescriptive
    C. Environmental/aesthetic
    D. Human-services

    3.____

4. In most public park and recreation departments, the largest area of use for volunteer workers is in

    A. direct leadership of groups or assisting professional leaders at work
    B. specialized educational appointments
    C. clerical assistance and helping with mailings, reports, and similar assignments
    D. administrative, promotional, or advisory activities

    4.____

5. The use of night lighting at outdoor recreational facilities typically creates each of the following benefits EXCEPT

    A. deterring personal crime
    B. overall lower cost per hour of public use
    C. beautification of the park by enhancing plants, trees, and architectural features
    D. distinguishing activities within the park

    5.____

6. Of the four types of in-service training administered to entry-level park and recreation employees, which is most likely to be delivered on an individual basis?

    6.____

A. General career development
B. Training to keep the worker up to date
C. Orientation to the job
D. Training related specifically to the position for which the employee was selected

7. In recent years, community leisure-service organizations have adopted each of the following methods for achieving a high degree of productivity and efficiency EXCEPT

    A. cost-cutting practices
    B. zero-based budgeting
    C. a more extensive use of cost-benefit analysis
    D. reduced contracting, concession, and leasing arrangements

8. Which of the following statements concerning contributory negligence and children is TRUE?
   A child
     I. under 7 years of age is conclusively adjudged to be incapable of contributory negligence
     II. between 7 and 10 years of age is rebuttably presumed to be incapable of negligence
     III. over fourteen years of age is presumed capable of negligence
   The CORRECT answer is:

    A. I only   B. I, II   C. I, III   D. II, III

9. In general, a daily program schedule is divided into blocks of time, with major blocks of time of an hour or more per block incorporated. Generally, the daily program schedule is arranged with

    A. one block of time scheduled in the morning and one in the afternoon
    B. one in the morning and two in the afternoon
    C. only one major block per day, usually in the morning
    D. only one major block per day, usually in the afternoon

10. The MAIN advantage of an unstructured, decentralized approach to recreational programming is

    A. being able to respond to local neighborhood needs and special characteristics
    B. a set of core activities that meet clear program guidelines
    C. more intimate contact between community members and recreational leaders
    D. more efficient use of personnel resources

11. According to the Management-by-Objectives model (MBO), which of the following is NOT a guideline for the setting of park and recreation agency objectives?

    A. Objectives must be broad and open to interpretation by evaluators.
    B. Personnel at each level should play a role in setting their own objectives.
    C. A limited number of major objectives should be used for each unit or individual.
    D. Each objective should be given a precise time limit for accomplishment.

12. Which of the following steps in the purchasing process of a public agency would typically occur FIRST?

    A. Justification
    B. Bids
    C. Specifications
    D. Purchase orders

13. Of the various types of fees and charges at their disposal, public recreation and park departments most often use

    A. entrance/admission fees
    B. lease revenue
    C. program/activity fees
    D. rental fees

14. When a park and recreation official has the opportunity to speak with the media about the operations of the department, he or she should

    A. speak in 30-second quotes, or shorter
    B. use technical language that will show the significance of the project or organization
    C. dress in bright colors
    D. use preface remarks

15. Each of the following is an advantage associated with contracting out various functions of a public park and recreation department EXCEPT

    A. greater departmental independence
    B. avoiding the restrictions of bureaucratic structures and similar political institutions
    C. lower personnel costs
    D. clearer contractual specification of quantity, quality, and price of work

16. Which of the following is NOT a growing trend in the personnel assignment policies of larger park and recreation departments?

    A. Having a fixed number of full-time, year-round employees supplemented by a limited number of specialists during the year, and an influx of summer workers for playground or camping programs
    B. Greater responsibility of *face-to-face* leaders in coordinating and directing programs
    C. Assignment of leaders to other district- or city-wide roles which can be carried out during slack periods
    D. Rotation of assignments at different seasons

17. According to most current practices in public agencies, the first work sessions on the departmental budget for the following year are generally held in the months of

    A. March-April
    B. May-June
    C. August-September
    D. October-November

18. Which of the following appears to have the LEAST significant effect on a person's opportunities to engage in recreational activities?

    A. Time
    B. Geographic and environmental resources
    C. Motivation
    D. Health and fitness

19. A park and recreation department's _____ is a document that includes planned and proposed expenditures for carrying out major purchases and construction projects of a substantial and long-term nature.

    A. operating budget
    B. balance sheet
    C. capital budget
    D. performance budget

    19._____

20. A large park of several hundred acres will generally provide _____ acres of area for every user.

    A. 1-2 B. 5 C. 10 D. 20

    20._____

21. Concerning intramural and extramural sports programs, most park and recreation departments have specific policies designed to deal with the issue of forfeited contests. Which of the following is NOT generally one of these policies?

    A. A team or individual not ready to play within thirty minutes after the scheduled time is charged with a forfeit.
    B. An individual or team may be assessed a forfeit fee.
    C. Two forfeits result in the elimination of an individual or team from all further participation in that sport.
    D. If a team or individual leaves before the forfeit is duly noted by an official or supervisor, then both teams should be charged with a forfeit.

    21._____

22. Most local park and recreation agencies function within a framework of legislation provided by the

    A. federal government
    B. state government
    C. municipal government
    D. appointed board

    22._____

23. Within a working group assigned to a specific task, the task structure is measured by each of the following EXCEPT the degree to which

    A. members understand what the goal is
    B. the correctness of a decision can be demonstrated by authority or logic
    C. multiple paths to the goal are evident
    D. one solution is more correct

    23._____

24. During a summer recreation program, quiet activities are usually BEST scheduled for

    A. as late in the day as possible
    B. the early afternoon
    C. mid-day
    D. the early morning

    24._____

25. Which of the following statements about adolescent recreationists is FALSE?

    A. They generally show a rapid increase in lung capacity.
    B. They are capable not only of describing, but of explaining situations or phenomena.
    C. Norms for male or female behavior are generally discovered through interactions with the opposite sex.
    D. They are concerned with the meaning of life according to religious and philosophical perspectives.

    25._____

KEY (CORRECT ANSWERS)

1. C
2. D
3. C
4. A
5. B

6. C
7. D
8. C
9. B
10. A

11. A
12. A
13. C
14. A
15. A

16. A
17. B
18. C
19. C
20. B

21. A
22. B
23. C
24. C
25. C

TEST 2

DIRECTIONS: Each question or incomplete statement is followed by several suggested answers or completions. Select the one that BEST answers the question or completes the statement. *PRINT THE LETTER OF THE CORRECT ANSWER IN THE SPACE AT THE RIGHT.*

1. In developing any recreation program, an administrator's primary emphasis is nearly always on

    A. education for leisure
    B. providing organized or supervised activities
    C. coordinating and assisting functions
    D. providing facilities for unscheduled and unsupervised use

    1.____

2. Each of the following is a disadvantage associated with the use of air-supported structures as a housing for recreational facilities EXCEPT

    A. their susceptibility to vandalism
    B. their short life expectancy
    C. lack of flexibility in yearly program scheduling
    D. possible zoning law conflicts

    2.____

3. Typically, which of the following would be the final step in the development of a maintenance management plan for a recreational facility?
The

    A. definition of the maintenance plan's overall goals and objectives
    B. development of work order request forms for non-routine, nonrecurring maintenance tasks
    C. creation of a format for scheduling maintenance work
    D. development of a form for daily maintenance work and assignments

    3.____

4. In liability terms, each of the following is a means of risk reduction for a park and recreation department EXCEPT

    A. conducting periodic safety inspections for all facilities and equipment
    B. training all employees in safety practices, first aid, and preventive maintenance
    C. clearly labeling potential risks to users
    D. developing safety rules for the operation of facilities and equipment

    4.____

5. Managing a public park and recreation department like a business, using marketing strategies, has proven effective for many departments in trimming costs and streamlining services, but the marketing approach does have several disadvantages. Which of the following is NOT generally considered to be one of them?

    A. The bottom line of program development is profitability.
    B. Efforts at securing public subsidies are likely to be reduced.
    C. Services to poorer community residents may atrophy.
    D. Possible ventures may be evaluated only in terms of who will be able to pay for them.

    5.____

6. The need for public relations in the field of parks and recreation is enforced by certain prevailing public attitudes. Which of the following is NOT generally considered to be one of these prevailing attitudes?

    A. Frequent occasions, brought about by the very nature of park and recreation operations, when individual citizens become irritated, frustrated, or disappointed
    B. Limited knowledge of the range of services and programs offered
    C. A generalized opposition to public funding of a department that is not considered to be part of the infrastructure
    D. The feeling that public recreation is not really a necessity; that the public is able to meet its leisure needs independently

6.____

7. In most states, the statute of limitations for litigating actions involving negligence is

    A. 1 year
    B. 2 years
    C. 10 years
    D. in most states, there is no statute of limitations

7.____

8. In park and recreation management applications, a *diagraph* is used to

    A. view the community-wide availability of programs and detect under- or over-provision of different types of activities on a geographical basis
    B. show all events or continuing activities in a convenient and easily understood form
    C. show individual projects or programs laid out along a calendar, with specific tasks indicated for the dates on which they are to be begun and completed
    D. identify major facilities and ongoing programs

8.____

9. Which of the following is considered to be the responsibility of a program-administrative staff member at a park and recreation department?

    A. Monitoring personnel practices
    B. Preparing statistical or analytical reports of operations
    C. Monitoring facility use and operations
    D. Implementing policies for safety

9.____

10. The probationary period for most newly-hired park and recreation personnel is

    A. 24-48 hours   B. 4-6 weeks
    C. 3-6 months   D. 1-2 years

10.____

11. For busy community members who have fluctuating schedules, and who want to compete in a more structured competitive environment, a recreation and park department's most effective way of dealing with competitive sports such as tennis is to establish a _____ tournament structure for participants.

    A. single elimination   B. double elimination
    C. challenge   D. round-robin

11.____

12. A specific tax leveled against the assessed value of residential or industrial property, the amount of which is assigned directly to the public park and recreation fund and used exclusively for that purpose, is known as a(n) _____ tax.

    A. millage   B. real estate
    C. impact   D. levy

12.____

13. A _____ approach to leisure service sees recreation not as an activity carried on for its own sake, but as designed to accomplish specific therapeutic goals.

    A. human-services
    B. marketing
    C. individualist
    D. prescriptive

14. Which of the following steps in the development of a park and recreation program is typically administered first?

    A. Establishing goals, objectives, and policies
    B. Identifying the range of possible activities and services
    C. Assessing participant or community needs and interests
    D. Developing a program plan

15. The growing trend in park and recreation departmental budgeting is toward the use of _____ budgets.

    A. program
    B. function classification
    C. performance
    D. line-item

16. What type of accounting system shows, on updated expenditure reports, all encumbrances or charges against specified accounts?

    A. Balance sheet
    B. Concurrent auditing
    C. Work program auditing
    D. Accrual

17. Which of the following statements about recreationists in middle childhood (6-12 years) is generally TRUE?

    A. Their muscles develop in function, but are still immature in size and strength.
    B. They have not mastered the concept of numbers, clock time, or calendar time.
    C. They do not exhibit abstract thought processes.
    D. They know rules which specify right from wrong, but may not understand the reasoning behind them.

18. Which of the following is NOT a typical benefit associated with informal structures and processes within the framework of a park and recreation department?

    A. Enhancement of a manager's authority
    B. Reduced time requirements for developing projects
    C. Increased opportunity for lower-level personnel to share meaningfully in agency planning
    D. Improved planning and problem-solving functions

19. Which of the following administration philosophies or strategies is NOT part of the future-oriented trend in park and recreation management?

    A. Evaluating services in terms of human consequences
    B. Offering programs anywhere in the community, with staff resources helping residents develop their own leadership skills
    C. Funding all basic programs from tax allocations
    D. Acting in an enabling or catalyzing role in matching community resources to citizen's needs

20. When a recreation and park manager has news of interest to the local newspaper, there are several approaches he or she might take. Which of the following should be used most sparingly?

    A. Arranging a news conference and invite interested reporters and editors
    B. Calling the newspaper, summarizing the information briefly to the appropriate editor or reporter, and allowing the person to suggest a course of action
    C. Writing the information in the form of a *letter to the editor* and mail or deliver it to the editor
    D. Preparing a news release and mail or deliver it to the editor

21. Each of the following is a typical policy used by park and recreation departments concerning the reservation of recreational facilities by community members EXCEPT

    A. cancellations must be made in person with the proper identification
    B. cancellations must be made 24 hours in advance, or a no-show penalty will apply
    C. persons absent 10 minutes past the reserved time forfeit all rights to the facility
    D. reservations must be made at least 4 hours in advance

22. In a departmental budget, the function of a work program is *primarily* to

    A. determine scheduling needs for the coming year
    B. estimate personnel expenditures
    C. establish a clear set of administrative performance standards
    D. outline tasks to be performed, standards of service and efficiency, and methods to be used

23. While conducting a needs assessment of the community, park and recreation administrators relate the leisure services currently offered to a set of national standards for such services in similar communities. In this situation, the administration is determining the community's _____ need for services.

    A. expressed   B. normative
    C. perceived   D. relative

24. Which of the following is not typically a heading used on a written maintenance plan for a recreational facility?

    A. Personnel   B. Chain of command
    C. Maintenance standards D. Frequency

25. According to the established national standard, a park and recreation manager who is planning a leisure facility should rely upon the figure of 1 acre of land needed for every _____ community residents.

    A. 100   B. 800   C. 1200   D. 2500

KEY (CORRECT ANSWERS)

1.	D	11.	C
2.	C	12.	A
3.	B	13.	D
4.	C	14.	C
5.	B	15.	A
6.	C	16.	D
7.	B	17.	D
8.	B	18.	A
9.	A	19.	C
10.	C	20.	A

21. D
22. D
23. B
24. B
25. B

EXAMINATION SECTION
TEST 1

DIRECTIONS: Each question or incomplete statement is followed by several suggested answers or completions. Select the one that BEST answers the question or completes the statement. *PRINT THE LETTER OF THE CORRECT ANSWER IN THE SPACE AT THE RIGHT.*

1. A *typical* definition of recreation agreed upon by MOST authorities would be
   A. voluntarily chosen leisure activities, for pleasure or personal benefit, meeting community standards and needs
   B. pleasurable activities provided by community agencies without social purpose
   C. whatever people want to do, because they want to do it
   D. purposeful activities, such as anti-delinquency, addiction treatment, or golden age programs, which make use of trips and cultural activities

1.____

2. In the past, it was argued that recreation programs for youth prevented juvenile delinquency.
Today the majority of social work or recreation authorities would MOST probably support the view that
   A. recreation is the key element in any anti-delinquency program
   B. recreation has proved to be of little value in anti-delinquency programs
   C. juvenile delinquents usually are anti-social and disruptive and should be kept out of organized recreation programs
   D. juvenile delinquency treatment requires varied services, including education, job training, recreation, and improved housing

2.____

3. The MAJOR professional organization serving the recreation field in the United States today is the
   A. American Institute of Park and Recreation Practitioners
   B. National Recreation and Park Association
   C. National Recreation Association
   D. American Association for Health, Physical Education, and Recreation

3.____

4. Varied theories of play have been developed by psychologists, philosophers, and others.
One TRADITIONAL theory that sees play as the means through which children prepare for the demands of adult life is the _____ theory.
   A. instinct-practice   B. catharsis
   C. recapitulation   D. relaxation

4.____

5. Which of the following statements BEST supports the self-expression theory of play as developed by Mason and Mitchell?
   A. Activities are engaged in for the purpose of overcoming natural human inertness.

5.____

B. Due to the pressures for self-maintenance and other compulsions, human beings use play as outlets for frustration.
C. Human physiological and anatomical structure are independent of any specific form of play.
D. Because human beings are dynamic animals, activity is a primary need of life.

6. Of the following, the MOST recent psychological theory of play is the 6.____
   A. pleasure principle theory (Freud)
   B. play extraversion theory (Piaget)
   C. arousal or stimulation theory (Berlynne)
   D. aggressive-release theory (Schiller-Spencer-Groos)

7. Generally, the BASIC philosophy of public recreation departments today is to 7.____
   A. serve all groups as fully as possible
   B. place the greatest emphasis on helping the poor
   C. serve primarily the middle and upper classes
   D. concentrate on children and youth

8. The one of the following which is NOT a widely accepted goal of public recreation departments is to 8.____
   A. provide constructive and creative outlets for leisure
   B. meet participants' physical, mental, social, and creative needs
   C. develop large numbers of athletes to play on college or pro teams
   D. strengthen family life and help community unity

9. The growth of the organized recreation movement in the United States was promoted by several social factors. 9.____
   Of the following, the one which did NOT contribute to such growth is
   A. the increase in leisure through the shortened work-week, more holidays, and longer vacations
   B. the development of movies, television, and radio as major forms of entertainment
   C. the general affluence and mobility in society
   D. more liberal attitudes toward leisure on the part of religious, educational, and government authorities

10. Recognition by state certifying boards or departments is one of the formal methods through which professionals in fields such as law or medicine are approved. 10.____
    Today, certification for recreation professionals exists in
    A. a small number of states   B. all fifty states
    C. no states   D. about half the states

11. Supervisors should be able to advise recently appointed recreation workers on the appropriate selection of activities for specific age groups. 11.____
    When planning for after-school recreation activities for boys of elementary-school age, the MOST useful type of game would usually be

A. low-organized games, such as dodge-ball, kick-ball, and relays
B. table games, such as parcheessi, backgammon, and chess
C. encounter games and touching games, like those used in sensitivity groups
D. mental games and contests, such as ghost, coffee-pot, and twenty questions

12. Since anti-social youth are often unwilling to enter highly structured activities and programs, or may be barred from recreation centers, they are frequently not served by community recreation agencies.
Of the following, the BEST way to serve such youth is to
    A. develop entirely new kinds of activities that will appeal to delinquents because of their thrill-seeking nature
    B. organize special community center programs to serve only delinquent youth who have been in trouble with the law
    C. assign roving or street gang workers to make contact with unaffiliated youth and gangs to involve them in constructive activities
    D. wait until they are sent to correctional institutions and then give them concentrated recreation programs there

12.____

13. Adolescent girls in youth houses (detention or remand centers) often have poor self-concepts.
Of the following, the TYPICAL approach used by recreation workers in such settings to help these girls improve their self-concepts is to
    A. tell such girls at appropriate times that they are just as good as anybody
    B. organize self-improvement classes to teach skills in make-up, dressing, or modeling
    C. sponsor sports teams, such as basketball or volleyball, which can compete with other institutions
    D. administer personality tests to diagnose their problems

13.____

14. Many teenage boys are fascinated by automobiles.
Of the following, a USEFUL way for a creation worker to deal with this interest would be to
    A. sponsor drag-racing meets in a conveniently located park or raceway
    B. develop an automotive hobby car repair club in a community center or nearby garage
    C. arrange a contest to select one boy to go on a trip to the Indianapolis 500 to watch the big race
    D. develop a joint program with a school bus company to train boys as junior bus operators

14.____

15. According to the traditional *space standards* employed for the past several decades to measure the need for open space and recreation facilities in American communities, there should be AT LEAST
    A. one neighborhood playground for each 1,500 children under age 12
    B. three acres of outdoor recreation space for each 1,000 residents
    C. one acre of outdoor recreation space for each 100 residents
    D. one community center for each 5,000 children and teenagers

15.____

16. *Therapeutic recreation service* is the term applied today to programs which serve the physically, mentally, or socially handicapped.
    For BEST results, such programs should be provided in
    A. institutions such as mental hospitals or schools for the mentally handicapped
    B. community settings such as after-care centers or community programs for the physically disabled
    C. both institutional and community settings
    D. private or voluntary facilities

16._____

17. Social group work is BEST defined as a method of social work which
    A. assigns people to groups for intensive psychotherapy as a means of crisis intervention
    B. helps people improve their social functioning and ability to cope with interpersonal problems
    C. utilizes unskilled community people to take over many social work organizations
    D. relies on the leader's ability to mobilize people into effective instruments for community reform

17._____

18. Some recreation departments operate multi-service senior centers which provide social services related to nutrition, health needs, legal, or housing assistance, as well as recreation.
    This type of program is regarded by leading authorities in the field of recreation as
    A. usually not the function of a recreation department since it has proved to be a hindrance to customary social and recreational programs
    B. clearly not the function of a recreation department and should be discontinued
    C. an appropriate function of a recreation department and is justified by Federal funding guidelines in this field
    D. an appropriate function of a recreation department only when the program is receiving a grant from the State Department of Aging

18._____

19. The view that MOST social workers generally have of recreation is that it is
    A. almost identical to social work
    B. a competitor with social work for public funds
    C. a medium through which they can involve and work constructively with participants
    D. strictly for fun, without a serious purpose

19._____

20. The three MAJOR areas of social work training and practice are
    A. group work, psychiatric case work, and neighborhood management
    B. community analysis, case work, and agency supervision
    C. group rehabilitation, psychiatric community development, and case work
    D. case work, group work, and community organization

20._____

21. Which of the following BEST expresses the program objectives of recreation programs provided by the municipal agencies as a whole?
They should
    A. emphasize after-school and summer vacation play programs
    B. provide activities for various age groups
    C. concentrate on programs for younger boys and teenage youth
    D. meet social needs that are unsatisfied by family relationships

22. Of the following, which is the LEAST appropriate basis for choosing the recreation program activities for a community center, hospital, or other institutions? The
    A. needs and interests of the participants based on their age, sex, socio-economic background, etc.
    B. overall philosophy and goals of the sponsoring agency
    C. ability of the agency to offer certain activities based on its staff resources, facilities, funding, etc.
    D. degree to which prospective participants are personally acquainted with one another

23. The MOST common approach to developing schedules of program activities in municipal recreation departments is to organize them
    A. on a centralized basis, that is, each central office or county headquarters develops a precise schedule that must be followed in each center or playground
    B. on a *report* system, that is, each center or playground develops its individual schedule and must report daily on which activities were carried out, and which were not
    C. on the basis of seasonal interests, with different schedules being developed for summer, fall, winter, and spring
    D. according to whatever seems to be of interest on a particular day, emphasizing flexibility

24. A difficult problem in scheduling recreation programs is to have personnel available at needed times.
The BEST approach for dealing with this problem is to
    A. change recreation leadership jobs to the four-day workweek that has become so popular in industry
    B. make leadership assignment schedules more flexible to insure coverage for special events, including evening and weekend activities
    C. assign all personnel a noon-to-8 P.M. daily schedule
    D. convert all full-time leadership jobs into part-time per session positions and then assign these as needed

25. Ideally, the BEST program schedule for a community recreation center would be one which covers
    A. the full day and evening to permit scheduling for senior citizens, housewives, or pre-schoolers, as well as youth and other adults
    B. from 3:00 P.M. to 10:00 P.M. since this is the time when children and youth are out of school

C. the daily hours of maximum use, based on participant demand, because of the financial limitations of many centers
D. daytime hours only since most people today will not come out at night because of fear of crime

---

KEY (CORRECT ANSWERS)

1.	A		11.	A
2.	D		12.	C
3.	B		13.	B
4.	A		14.	B
5.	D		15.	C
6.	C		16.	C
7.	A		17.	B
8.	C		18.	C
9.	B		19.	C
10.	A		20.	D

21.	B
22.	D
23.	C
24.	B
25.	A

TEST 2

DIRECTIONS: Each question or incomplete statement is followed by several suggested answers or completions. Select the one that BEST answers the question or completes the statement. *PRINT THE LETTER OF THE CORRECT ANSWER IN THE SPACE AT THE RIGHT.*

1. Active team games during the summer months of July and August at a neighborhood playground are BEST scheduled for
   A. early afternoon and late evening
   B. Saturday only (morning and afternoon)
   C. morning, late afternoon, and evening
   D. evening only (after 7:30 P.M.

   1.____

2. Various activities help to keep attendance at a summer playground high by building interest and enthusiasm among participants.
   Which of the following is the POOREST example of such activities?
   A. Weekly special events, such as pet shows, bicycle rodeos, hobby fairs, etc.
   B. End-of-summer festivals, carnivals, play-days, exhibitions, etc., for which participants prepare for several weeks
   C. Trips using chartered or public transportation to state parks, swimming pools, etc. for those attending regularly
   D. Daily tutoring programs of remedial education for those who are having difficulty in school

   2.____

3. Of the various types of activities sponsored by public recreation departments, the MOST popular single category, according to national surveys, is
   A. services for the handicapped (such as the mentally handicapped, blind, or physical disabled)
   B. the performing arts (music, drama, and dance)
   C. social activities (clubs, parties, dances, etc.)
   D. sports of all kinds (such as baseball, football, and basketball)

   3.____

4. The MOST typical method of organizing youth sports leagues in public recreation departments is to
   A. encourage recreation leaders to organize and coach several teams themselves, running their own tournaments
   B. reduce competitive play, which is harmful to youth, and concentrate instead on cooperative games
   C. work with community organizations that set up and coach their own teams
   D. have children on each block form their own teams and do their own coaching

   4.____

5. Each craft activity has a specific set of items describing its equipment or process. The following words, *bisque*, *greenware*, and *slab-construction*, are used in reference to
   A. ceramics   B. metalcrafts
   C. glass-blowing D. decoupage

   5.____

6. According to their degree of difficulty, various arts and crafts activities are usually suited to different age levels,
Which of the following would be MOST suited to pre-school children?
   A. Macrame
   B. Watercolor painting
   C. Fingerpainting
   D. Jewelry-making

6.____

7. Among the most popular recreational sport activities are basketball, baseball, and bowling.
The terms which do NOT apply to any of these three games are
   A. strike, dribble, sacrifice
   B. linebacker, offside, foot-fault
   C. spare, infield, hoop
   D. walking, infield, alley

7.____

8. Which of the following activities would LEAST likely be found in a municipal recreation department's music program?
   A. Rock-and-roll band practice and competition
   B. Chamber music groups
   C. Drum and bugle corps
   D. Informal community singing or folk music activities

8.____

9. Informal dramatics activities are often used with children and teenagers.
Which of the following would be MOST likely to promote creative dramatic skills and interest among beginners?
   A. One-act play contests with scripts, costumes, and scenery
   B. Choral reading of popular poetry
   C. Memorizing and reciting sections from famous Broadway plays
   D. Improvisational dramatic games, like prop or paper bag plays

9.____

10. In the past, many recreation departments sponsored holiday festivals or special events such as the English May Day Festival.
Today, the trend is to
   A. have such festivals reflect ethnic group interests such as Black Culture or Hispanic-American Arts
   B. eliminate all such events since there is little interest in them
   C. deal mainly with historical commemorations since these would appeal to traditional patriotism
   D. make festivals *future-minded* by dealing with the Space Age or America of the Future

10.____

11. Of the following types of tournaments, the type which can be completed MOST quickly in individual sports such as fencing or table-tennis is the _____ tournament.
   A. round robin
   B. elimination
   C. challenge (pyramid)
   D. challenge (ladder)

11.____

12. Recreation has been affected by several key trends in psychiatric treatment.
Which of the following is NOT such a key trend?
   A. Reducing patient populations in large, distant state institutions and setting up local mental health facilities, with after-care or day-clinic programs

12.____

B. Reliance on chemotherapy, which makes patients more receptive to programs
C. The development of activity therapy programs in many hospitals, which include education, recreation, occupational therapy, and similar activities
D. Hiring of psychiatric patients as recreation aides, which may lead to employment after discharge

13. In recreation programs serving the seriously physically handicapped, such as those who have suffered strokes, amputations, etc., the PRIMARY program objective is to
    A. help patients develop potential skills using the facilities of community and out-of-hospital recreational programs
    B. raise funds, through parties, bazaars, special shows, etc., that patients put on to meet special patient needs
    C. use recreation as a specific treatment modality that will restore function, help patients learn to use prosthesis, etc.
    D. make patients accept their limitations and the fact that they cannot participate in many normal recreation activities

13.____

14. The majority of mentally handicapped teenagers or young adults live in the community, rather than in institutions. Recreation for such persons has several important goals.
    Of the following, the LEAST appropriate recreation goal for such persons is to
    A. help them improve the poor coordination and overcome the obesity typical of many such persons through physical activity
    B. help them acquire social skills and improve behavior and appearance so they will be able to mingle with others more effectively
    C. provide enjoyable and socially desirable leisure activities in order to make life more satisfying
    D. improve their I.Q.'s in order to help them get better jobs or be able to continue in school

14.____

15. Senior centers that serve older persons should meet the important needs of these individuals.
    Of the following, it would be LEAST appropriate for such centers to meet the need for
    A. full-time employment by acting as a placement bureau for center members
    B. modified physical activity to help keep older people active and prevent physical deterioration
    C. social activity to help aging people make friends and avoid isolation
    D. program activities in which older people may do volunteer service in hospitals or in the community

15.____

16. In planning a recreation program at a low-income public housing project, it is important to establish an advisory board or council.
Such board or council should represent PRIMARILY the needs and interests of the
    A. civic groups
    B. residents
    C. parent-teacher associations
    D. youth workers

16.____

17. Public relations may have many objectives for a public recreation department. Of the following, the LEAST appropriate objective would be to
    A. provide accurate information about the department's overall program to the public at large
    B. encourage attendance and involvement at the department's events and regular programs
    C. build favorable public attitudes and encourage volunteer leadership in the programs
    D. encourage petitions or letter-writing campaigns for increased budgets for the department

17.____

18. The one of the following which is the MOST effective method for producing successful public relations is for recreation program administrators to
    A. appear before civil organizations
    B. satisfy users of programs
    C. publish effective brochures, announcements, and reports
    D. employ qualified, indigenous para-professionals

18.____

19. If a recreation supervisor were going to publicize a large one-day recreation event in his borough, the BEST way to promote attendance would be to
    A. use newspaper releases and distribute fliers to schools, churches, and temples
    B. place posters advertising the event in store windows
    C. put posters on playground bulletin boards
    D. make a filmstrip about the forthcoming event and distribute prints to civic groups

19.____

20. Assume that, as a recreation supervisor, you are directing a community center that has poor participation in programs by local residents.
Of the following, the MOST effective way for you to arouse more public interest would be to
    A. have the publicity office in your department's central office send out newspaper releases about the center
    B. form a neighborhood council to interpret the community's needs to you and help publicize your program
    C. frequent places where local people congregate
    D. plan a panel discussion in a nearby community auditorium to discuss the problem

20.____

21. There are several possible approaches to getting community involvement in recreation service.
Of the following, the approach that would usually be LEAST workable would be to

    A. draw up a list of interested parents, clergymen, businessmen, local educators, etc., and invite them to a planning meeting about the neighborhood's recreation program
    B. announce an election to a recreation council, and select a slate of nominees, one for each square block so that local residents can elect their own representatives
    C. inquire as to whether the local Parent-Teachers Association will form a subcommittee interested in youth recreation to assist you
    D. work closely with the local district planning board to insure that they consider recreation as an important community service and to get their advice and help

21.____

22. Whether patients will be able to use their leisure constructively after discharge from the hospital is of vital concern to recreation workers in psychiatric hospitals.
Which of the following approaches would be LEAST useful in assuring continuing recreation service to a patient?

    A. Get a mimeographed list of recreation agencies in a patient's neighborhood and give him this before he is discharged
    B. Visit and talk with staff members of recreation agencies in a patient's neighborhood to make plans for their receiving the discharged patient
    C. Develop joint hospital-community recreation programs in special events, tours, entertainment programs, etc. to build a base of understanding for discharged patients
    D. Help the patient develop skills and interests in activities that will actually be available in his neighborhood after discharge

22.____

23. Therapeutic recreation seeks to help disabled persons enjoy a fuller, happier life. The question of whether they should be segregated in separate programs for the handicapped is an important one.
Which of the following statements about this group is MOST valid?

    A. The non-handicapped in society are usually very sympathetic to the disabled and welcome them in all recreational and social programs.
    B. The handicapped are better off by themselves, in groups with others having similar disabilities, so they will not feel inferior.
    C. It is an important goal to integrate the handicapped with other persons whenever possible, although sometimes it may not be feasible.
    D. The handicapped should, without exception, be mixed with the non-handicapped in recreation programs.

23.____

24. Recreation is usually considered to be a positive force for improving social relations between different racial, ethnic, or socio-economic groups.
Of the following, which is the MOST valid statement about recreation and inter-group relations?

24.____

A. Public recreation is one field in which racial discrimination is not prohibited by law.
B. Recreation workers have an obligation to reflect and agree with the views of those they serve, regardless of the nature of such views.
C. Many of our community recreation programs are heavily racially segregated.
D. Prejudice is an inborn trait which often appears in competitive sports.

25. For minority-group youth, sports often provide upward social mobility into college and subsequent business careers.
However, of the following, a MAJOR problem that arises for such youth in their seeking upward social mobility is that
    A. unscrupulous college sports programs often exploit them
    B. they are unable to satisfactorily relate to members of their peer group
    C. sports fail to provide an outlet for hostility and aggression
    D. religious cults to which they become converted distract them from sports

KEY (CORRECT ANSWERS)

1.	C	11.	B
2.	D	12.	D
3.	D	13.	A
4.	C	14.	D
5.	A	15.	A
6.	C	16.	B
7.	B	17.	D
8.	B	18.	B
9.	D	19.	A
10.	A	20.	B

21.	B
22.	A
23.	C
24.	C
25.	A

TEST 3

DIRECTIONS: Each question or incomplete statement is followed by several suggested answers or completions. Select the one that BEST answers the question or completes the statement. *PRINT THE LETTER OF THE CORRECT ANSWER IN THE SPACE AT THE RIGHT.*

1. The trend in many recreation and park departments during the past several years has been toward providing special facilities and programs based on user fees and charges.
   The criticism MOST often made against such fees and charges is that
   A. few recreation directors have made serious efforts to serve residents of disadvantaged neighborhoods
   B. it increases the cost of servicing and maintaining facilities and services because standards must be raised
   C. public employees may be tempted to misappropriate funds or may be subject to accusations of dishonesty
   D. poor people may be unable to participate in what should be a publicly-available service

   1.____

2. With few exceptions, recreation directors have not been able to gain permission to operate programs regularly in school buildings.
   Of the following, the MOST successful way to improve this situation is to
   A. develop relationships and cooperative programs with local school board and district officials, or with individual school principals and custodians
   B. bring a class-action suit against the local schoolboard
   C. collect and submit legally valid petitions to the administration
   D. exert pressure on the schools by denying them use of parks or other recreational facilities for their physical education activities

   2.____

3. Many hospitals, particularly psychiatric hospitals, have therapists keep regular reports of patient participation in recreation programs.
   Of the following, the BEST use of such reports is to
   A. provide information which may be presented at meetings of the treatment team when the progress of patients is discussed
   B. provide a basis for a daily discussion between the patient and the therapist so the patient knows what is expected of him
   C. justify adverse actions such as denial of recreation privileges or the imposition of personal restrictions
   D. meet the requirements of mental hygiene laws as to standards of treatment and patient progress

   3.____

4. Much correspondence is likely to come into the central office of a public recreation department.
   Generally, all letters should be answered within one or two days UNLESS
   A. a letter is of a commonplace and unimportant nature
   B. the writer is unreasonably critical of the department
   C. form letters are used in place of personalized correspondence
   D. a letter requires special inquiries or decision-making

   4.____

5. One major type of report in recreation programs is based on the attendance of participants.
Such report are GENERALLY considered to be
   A. an excellent quantitative and qualitative basis for evaluating the success of a program
   B. of primary use in operational research involving participant behavior and outcomes
   C. unnecessary since few departments continue to use attendance reports as a basis for funding
   D. quite inaccurate unless attendance counts are done systematically and staff members avoid inflating them

6. An informal survey of recreation in a hospital showed that patients who engaged regularly in the program were discharged from the hospital earlier than those who did not.
Based on this information only, it would be MOST valid to say that
   A. such information has validity or meaning only to a qualified medical research person
   B. it is inconclusive whether there exists a cause and effect relationship between participation and discharge
   C. probably the healthier patients took part in the recreation program, and this was the reason for their earlier discharge
   D. recreation was the major determinant of earlier discharge

7. The one of the following it would be BEST to do when preparing or developing an annual report of a large recreational program is to
   A. gather material such as photos, program descriptions, news stories, and statistics which appeared during the courses of the year
   B. use narrative description rather than charts or graphs to present statistical data
   C. present only the positive aspects and successes of your program, elaborating when necessary to give a favorable picture
   D. give praise to key political figures in the report so they will support the program in the future

8. *Crash* programs of recreation have sometimes been rushed into slum areas as a response to the threat of violence. Often, the approach has been to present *portable* programs, for example, portable pools put into lots of streets, mobile libraries and nature displays, puppet shows, movies, and rock or soul music shows.
Of the following, the MAJOR weakness of the *portable* recreation approach is that
   A. funds expended for such programs tend to be excessive and the general public is antagonized
   B. it emphasizes expending aimless energy rather than promoting social growth
   C. it meets only temporary recreation needs and fails to effect a permanent resolution of recreation problems

D. it tends to draw large numbers of youth out on the street, where they become riotous

9. A recent change in the concept of recreation as a public service is that it is now being thought of as a kind of social therapy.
   The MOST recent illustration of this has been the
   A. joint effort of religious agencies to develop new recreation programs, including year-round camping, for broken families
   B. expanded recreation programs in youth houses, remand institutions, and similar institutions run by the Department of Social Services
   C. new recreation program in private or multi-room occupancy hotels
   D. crash effort to provide recreation programs for alcoholics and older drug addicts

9.____

10. Low-income and racial minority youth tend to have very limited recreation interests. Often, teenage boys want to take part in basketball, but little else of an organized nature.
    For a recreation center director, what would be the BEST professional approach to this attitude?
    A. Begin with the interests they already have, then try to broaden their involvement in other recreation, athletic, or cultural activities
    B. Stick to basketball, their true interest, since they resist other activities
    C. Since they are able to play basketball in many neighborhood settings, eliminate this part of the program and offer new kinds of sports, cultural activities, and social events
    D. Rely on carefully prepared interest survey, and then offer youth only the activities and events they say they want

10.____

11. A NEW trend in many cities, with respect to the assignment of recreation leadership personnel, is to
    A. assign workers to one setting on a full-time, year-round basis so that they will be completely familiar with the work and do a superior job
    B. use seniority more than ever before, thereby giving the long-time employee freedom to pick his job
    C. rotate the assignments of workers from season-to-season or even day-to-day maximize output and improve morale by giving challenging assignments
    D. create new job shifts, such as one week from 9:00 to 5:00, next week from 2:00 to 10:00, etc.

11.____

12. Recreation counseling is becoming more widely used in many hospitals. Such counseling is PRIMARILY intended to
    A. help patients explore their leisure attitudes and interests and motivate them toward fuller participation after discharge
    B. teach patients a broad range of activities, such as sports, crafts, and social skills, that they can use after discharge
    C. use the recreation situation to uncover problems that can then be discussed when the patient gets therapeutic counseling

12.____

D. allow the patients to advise staff members on how best to organize the recreation program

13. A major problem today in many recreation and park departments is costly and destructive vandalism.
Which of the following methods of dealing with this problem has NOT been widely accepted throughout the United States?
    A. Provide stronger enforcement of rules and better surveillance and protection of recreation and park facilities
    B. Offer more attractive programs since people are less likely to vandalize a facility if it is staffed and providing popular community activities
    C. Use new types of designs so that facilities are less prone to vandalism, such as windowless buildings, concrete benches and tables, etc.
    D. Abandon parks or playgrounds that have been repeatedly vandalized

13.____

14. The Board of Education has a strong commitment to recreation.
Its recreation program focuses CHIEFLY on
    A. adult education programs in adult centers
    B. children and youth in after-school and evening centers
    C. the categories of pre-school, mentally handicapped, and senior citizens
    D. youth either considered to be pre-delinquent or adjudicated as delinquent

14.____

15. Those working to provide recreation to persons who have a physical, mental, emotional, or social disability frequently seek assistance from social service agencies.
Which of the following pairs of agencies is LEAST likely to be helpful to them?
    A. Catholic Charities; Federation of Protestant Welfare Agencies
    B. United Cerebral Palsy of N.Y.C.; New York Association for the Blind
    C. New York Association for Retarded Children; National Wheelchair Athletic Association
    D. New York League for Crippled and Disabled Children, Adults and Aging; Handclasp for the Handicapped, Inc.

15.____

16. Throughout the nation, there has been an increase in senior centers for aging persons.
Which of the following agencies does NOT sponsor special centers for aging persons?
    A. Housing Authority's low-income projects
    B. Office of Continuing Education
    C. Parks, Recreation and Cultural Affairs Administration
    D. Department of Social Services

16.____

17. The municipal department that has the PRIMARY responsibility for providing social services for youth, including recreation, is the
    A. Youth Activities Board
    B. Youth Services Agency
    C. United Block Association for Youth
    D. Bureau of Youth Community Services

17.____

18. If a recreation center director had severe problems with drug users in his neighborhood, the APPROPRIATE municipal department for him to ask for assistance is the
    A. Health and Hospitals Corporation
    B. Syanon or Phoenix House
    C. Department of Correction
    D. Addiction Services Agency

Questions 19-20.

DIRECTIONS: Questions 19 and 20 are to be answered SOLELY on the basis of the following passage.

This country was built on the puritanical belief that honest toil was the foundation of moral rectitude, the cement of society, and the uphill road to progress. Idleness was sin. As a result, we treat free time today as a conditional joy. We permit ourselves to relax only as a reward for hard work or as the recreation needed to put us back into shape for the job. Thus, the aimless delightful play of children gives way in adult life to a serious dedication to golf, the game that is so good for business.

19. According to the above passage, during former times in this country, respectable work was considered to be MOST NEARLY a
    A. way to improve health   B. form of recreation
    C. developer of good character D. reward for leisure

20. According to the point of view presented in the above passage, it would be MOST reasonable to assume that an employer would consider an employee's vacation to be a time for the employee to
    A. determine his own leisure time priorities
    B. loaf and relax
    C. learn new recreational skills
    D. increase his effectiveness at work

Questions 21-23.

DIRECTIONS: Questions 21 through 23 are to be answered SOLELY on the basis of the following passage.

One of the key supervisory problems in a large municipal recreation department is that many leaders are assigned to isolated playgrounds or small centers, where it is difficult to observe their work regularly. Often their facilities are extremely limited. In such settings, as well as in larger recreation centers, where many recreation leaders tend to have other jobs as well, there tends to be a low level of morale and incentive. Still, it is the supervisor's task to help recreation personnel to develop pride in their work, and to maintain a high level of performance. With isolated leaders, the supervisor may give advice or assistance. Leaders may be assigned to different tasks or settings during the year to maximize their productivity and provide new challenges. When it is clear that leaders are not willing to make a real effort to contribute to the department, the possibility of penalties must be considered, within the scope of departmental policy and the union contract. However, the supervisor should be constructive, encourage and assist workers to take a greater interest in their work, be innovative, and try to raise morale and to improve performance in positive ways.

21. The one of the following that would be the MOST appropriate title for the foregoing passage is
    A. SMALL COMMUNITY CENTERS – PRO AND CON
    B. PLANNING BETTER RECREATION PROGRAMS
    C. THE SUPERVISOR'S TASK IN UPGRADING PERSONNEL PERFORMANCE
    D. THE SUPERVISOR AND THE MUNICIPAL UNION – RIGHTS AND OBLIGATIONS

21.____

22. The above passage makes clear that recreation leadership performance in ALL recreation playgrounds and centers throughout a large city is
    A. generally above average, with good morale on the part of most recreation leaders
    B. beyond description since no one has ever observed or evaluated leaders
    C. a key test of the personnel department's effort to develop more effective hiring standards
    D. of mixed quality, with many recreation leaders having poor morale and a low level of achievement

22.____

23. According to the above passage, the supervisor's role is to
    A. use disciplinary action as his major tool in upgrading performance
    B. tolerate the lack of effort of individual employees since they are assigned to isolated playgrounds or small centers
    C. employ encouragement, advice, and, when appropriate, disciplinary action to improve performance
    D. inform the county supervisor whenever malfeasance or idleness is detected

23.____

Questions 24-25.

DIRECTIONS: Questions 24 and 25 are to be answered SOLELY on the basis of the following passage.

A recent study revealed some very concrete evidence concerning the relationship between avocations and mental health. A number of well-adjusted persons were surveyed as to the type, number, and duration of their hobbies. The findings were compared to those from a similar survey of mentally disturbed persons. In the well-adjusted group, both the number of hobbies and the intensity with which they were pursued were far greater than that of the mentally disturbed group.

24. According to the above passage, the study showed that
    A. well-adjusted people engage in hobbies more widely and deeply than do mentally disturbed people
    B. hobbies, if taken seriously, serve to keep most people mentally well

24.____

C. mental patients should be taught hobbies as a part of their therapy
D. the degree of interest in hobbies plays an important role in maintaining good mental health

25. In reference to the study mentioned in the above passage, it is MOST accurate to say that it appears to have 25._____
    A. been based on a carefully-structured, complex research design
    B. considered the variables of mental health and hobby involvement
    C. contained a general definition of mental health
    D. given evidence of a causal relationship between hobbies and mental health

---

KEY (CORRECT ANSWERS)

1.	D	11.	C
2.	A	12.	A
3.	A	13.	D
4.	D	14.	B
5.	D	15.	D
6.	B	16.	B
7.	A	17.	B
8.	C	18.	D
9.	B	19.	C
10.	A	20.	D

21. C
22. D
23. C
24. A
25. B

EXAMINATION SECTION
TEST 1

DIRECTIONS: Each question or incomplete statement is followed by several suggested answers or completions. Select the one that BEST answers the question or completes the statement. *PRINT THE LETTER OF THE CORRECT ANSWER IN THE SPACE AT THE RIGHT.*

1. Good procedure in handling complaints from the public may be divided into the following four principal stages:
   I. Investigation of the complaint
   II. Receipt of the complaint
   III. Assignment of responsibility for investigation and correction
   IV. Notification of correction

   The ORDER in which these stages ordinarily come is:
   A. III, II, I, IV   B. II, III, I, IV   C. II, III, IV, I   D. II, IV, III, I

   1.____

2. The department may expect the MOST severe public criticism if
   A. it asks for an increase in its annual budget
   B. it purchases new and costly street cleaning equipment
   C. sanitation officers and men are reclassified to higher salary grades
   D. there is delay in cleaning streets of snow

   2.____

3. The MOST important function of public relations in the department should be to
   A. develop cooperation on the part of the public in keeping streets clean
   B. get stricter penalties enacted for health code violations
   C. recruit candidates for entrance positions who ca be developed into supervisors
   D. train career personnel so that they can advance in the department

   3.____

4. The one of the following which has MOST frequently elicited unfavorable public comment has been
   A. dirty sidewalks or streets   B. dumping on lot
   C. failure to curb dogs   D. overflowing garbage cans

   4.____

5. It has been suggested that, as a public relations measure, sections hold *open house* for the public.
   The MOST effective time for this would be
   A. during the summer when children are not in school and can accompany their parents
   B. during the winter when show is likely to fall and the public can see snow removal preparations
   C. immediately after a heavy snow storm when department snow removal operations are in full progress
   D. when street sanitation is receiving general attention as during *Keep City Clean* week

   5.____

6. When a public agency conducts a public relations program, it is MOST likely to find that each recipient of its message will
   A. disagree with the basic purpose of the message if the officials are not well known to him
   B. accept the message if it is presented by someone perceived as having a definite intention to persuade
   C. ignore the message unless it is presented in a literate and clever manner
   D. give greater attention to certain portions of the message as a result of his individual and cultural differences

7. Following are three statements about public relations and communications:
   I. A person who seeks to influence public opinion can speed up a trend
   II. Mass communications is the exposure of a mass audience to an idea
   III. All media are equally effective in reaching opinion leaders
   Which of the following choices CORRECTLY classifies the above statements into those which are correct and those which are not?
   A. I and II are correct, but III is not.
   B. II and III are correct, but I is not.
   C. I and III are correct, but II is not.
   D. III is correct, but I and II are not.

8. Public relations experts say that MAXIMUM effect for a message results from
   A. concentrating in one medium
   B. ignoring mass media and concentrating on *opinion makers*
   C. presenting only those factors which support a given position
   D. using a combination of two or more of the available media

9. To assure credibility and avoid hostility, the public relations man MUST
   A. make certain his message is truthful, not evasive or exaggerated
   B. make sure his message contains some dire consequence if ignored
   C. repeat the message often enough so that it cannot be ignored
   D. try to reach as many people and groups as possible

10. The public relations man MUST be prepared to assume that members of his audience
    A. may have developed attitudes toward his proposals—favorable, neutral, or unfavorable
    B. will be immediately hostile
    C. will consider his proposals with an open mind
    D. will invariably need an introduction to his subject

11. The one of the following statements that is CORRECT is:
    A. When a stupid question is asked of you by the public, it should be disregarded
    B. If you insist on formality between you and the public, the public will not be able to ask stupid questions that cannot be answered
    C. The public should be treated courteously, regardless of how stupid their questions may be
    D. You should explain to the public how stupid their questions are

12. With regard to public relations, the MOST important item which should be emphasized in an employee training program is that
    A. each inspector is a public relations agent
    B. an inspector should give the public all the information it asks for
    C. it is better to make mistakes and give erroneous information than to tell the public that you do not know the correct answer to their problem
    D. public relations is so specialized a field that only persons specially trained in it should consider it

12.____

13. Members of the public frequently ask about departmental procedures.
    Of the following, it is BEST to
    A. advise the public to put the question in writing so that he can get a proper formal reply
    B. refuse to answer because this is a confidential matter
    C. explain the procedure as briefly as possible
    D. attempt to avoid the issue by discussing other matters

13.____

14. The effectiveness of a public relations program in a public agency such as the authority is BEST indicated by the
    A. amount of mass media publicity favorable to the policies of the authority
    B. morale of those employees who directly serve the patrons of the authority
    C. public's understanding and support of the authority's program and policies
    D. number of complaint received by the authority from patrons using its facilities

14.____

15. In an attempt to improve public opinion about a certain idea, the BEST course of action for an agency to take would be to present the
    A. clearest statements of the idea even though the language is somewhat technical
    B. idea as the result of long-term studies
    C. idea in association with something familiar to most people
    D. idea as the viewpoint of the majority leaders

15.____

16. The fundamental factor in any agency's community relations program is
    A. an outline of the objectives
    B. relations with the media
    C. the everyday actions of the employees
    D. a well-planned supervisory program

16.____

17. The FUNDAMENTAL factor in the success of a community relations program is
    A. true commitment by the community
    B. true commitment by the administration
    C. a well-planned, systematic approach
    D. the actions of individuals in their contacts with the public

17.____

18. The statement below which is LEAST correct is: 18.____
    A. Because of selection standards, the supervisor frequently encounters problems resulting from subordinates' inability to express themselves in the language of the profession.
    B. Distortion of the meaning of a communication is usually brought about by a failure to use language that has a precise meaning to others.
    C. The term *filtering* is the distortion or dilution of content of a communication that occurs as information is passed from individual to individual.
    D. The complexity of the *communications net* will directly affect.

19. Consider the following three statements that may or may not be CORRECT: 19.____
    I. In order to prevent the stifling of communications flow, supervisors should insist that employees use the formal communications network.
    II. Two-way communications are faster and more accurate than one-way communications.
    III. There is a direct correlation between the effectiveness of communications and the total setting in which they occur.
    The choice below which MOST accurately describes the above statement is:
    A. All three are correct.
    B. All three are incorrect.
    C. More than one statement is correct.
    D. Only one of the statements is correct.

20. The statement below which is MOST inaccurate is: 20.____
    A. The supervisor's most important tool in learning whether or not he is communicating well is feedback.
    B. Follow-up is essential if useful feedback is to be obtained.
    C. Subordinates are entitled, as a matter of right, to explanations from management concerning the reasons for orders or directives.
    D. A skilled supervisor is often able to use the grapevine to good advantage.

21. *Since concurrence by those affected is not sought, this kind of communication can be issued with relative ease.* 21.____
    The kind of communication being referred to in this quotation is
    A. autocratic   B. democratic   C. directive   D. free-rein

22. The statement below which is LEAST correct is: 22.____
    A. Clarity is more important in oral communicating than in written since the readers of a written communication can read it over again.
    B. Excessive use of abbreviations in written communications should be avoided.
    C. Short sentences with simple words are preferred over complex sentences and difficult words in a written communication.
    D. The *newspaper* style of writing ordinarily simplifies expression and facilitates understanding.

23. Which one of the following is the MOST important factor for the department to consider in building a good public image?
    A. A good working relationship with the news media
    B. An efficient community relations program
    C. An efficient system for handling citizen complaints
    D. The proper maintenance of facilities and equipment
    E. The behavior of individuals in their contacts with the public.

24. It has been said that the ability to communicate clearly and concisely is the MOST important single skill of the supervisor.
    Consider the following statements:
    I.   The adage, *Actions speak louder than words*, has NO application in superior/subordinate communications since good communications are accomplished with words.
    II. The environment in which a communication takes place will *rarely* determine its effect.
    III. Words are symbolic representations which must be associated with past experience or else they are meaningless.
    The choice below which MOST accurately describes the above statements is:
    A. I, II, and III are correct.
    B. I and II are correct, but III is not.
    C. I and III are correct, but II is not.
    D. III is correct, but I and II are not.
    E. I, II, and III are incorrect.

25. According to expert opinion, the effectiveness of an organization is very dependent upon good upward, downward, and lateral communications. Lateral communications are most important to the activity of coordinating the efforts of organizational units. Before real communication can take place at any level, barriers to communication must be recognized, understood, and removed.
    Consider the following three statements:
    I.   The *principal* barrier to good communications is a failure to establish empathy between sender and receiver.
    II. The difference in status or rank between the sender and receiver of a communication may be a communications barrier.
    III. Communications are easier if they travel upward from subordinate to superior
    The choice below which MOST accurately describes the above statements is:
    A. I, II and III are incorrect.   B. I and II are incorrect.
    C. I, II, and III are correct.   D. I and II are correct.
    E. I and III are incorrect.

KEY (CORRECT ANSWERS)

1. B
2. D
3. A
4. A
5. D

6. D
7. A
8. D
9. A
10. A

11. C
12. A
13. C
14. C
15. C

16. C
17. D
18. A
19. D
20. C

21. A
22. A
23. E
24. D
25. E

EXAMINATION SECTION
TEST 1

DIRECTIONS: Each question or incomplete statement is followed by several suggested answers or completions. Select the one that BEST answers the question or completes the statement. *PRINT THE LETTER OF THE CORRECT ANSWER IN THE SPACE AT THE RIGHT.*

1. A specialist is meeting with a panel of local community leaders to determine their perceptions about the effectiveness of a recent outreach program. The leaders seem unresponsive to the specialist's questions, looking at the floor or each other without directly answering the specialist's questions.
   One strategy that might work to elicit the desired information would be to
   A. try to discern the hidden meaning of their silence
   B. adopt a mildly confrontational tone and remind them of what's at stake in the community
   C. keep asking open-ended questions and wait patiently for responses
   D. tell them to come back when they're ready to tell you their opinions

1.____

2. Each of the following statements about maintaining a community's attention is true, EXCEPT:
   A. The more challenging it is to pay attention to a message, the more likely it is that it will be attended to
   B. Listeners will be more motivated to pay attention if a speech is personally meaningful
   C. People will be more likely to attend if a speaker pauses to suggest natural transitions in a speech
   D. Listeners will attend to messages that stand out

2.____

3. Each of the following is a key strategy to integrative bargaining among community members in conflict, EXCEPT
   A. focusing on positions, rather than interests
   B. separating the people from the problem
   C. aiming for an outcome based on an objectively identified standard
   D. using active listening skills, such as rephrasing and questioning

3.____

4. Which of the following is NOT one of the major variables to take into account when considering a community needs assessment?
   A. State of program development   B. Resources available
   C. Demographics   D. Community attitudes

4.____

5. Which of the following groups would probably be formed specifically for, or be involved in, the purpose of addressing a specific unmet community need?
   A. An existing consumer group
   B. A council of community representatives
   C. A committee
   D. An existing community organization

5.____

6. If a public outreach campaign designed to mobilize a community fails, the MOST likely reason for this failure is that the campaign
    A. was not specific about what it wanted people to do
    B. was overly serious and did not appeal to people's sense of humor
    C. offered no incentive for the audience to make a change
    D. did not use language that appealed to the audience's emotions

7. Nationwide, the rate of involvement of elderly people in community-based programs demonstrates that they are
    A. under-served when compared to other age groups
    B. served at about the same rate as other age groups
    C. over-served when compared to other age groups
    D. hardly served at all

8. In projecting the likelihood of an education program's success, a domestic violence specialist identifies every single event that must occur to complete the project. The specialist then arranges these events in sequential order and allocates time requirements for each. Finally, the total time is calculated and a model showing all their events and timelines is charted.
   The specialist has used
    A. a PERT chart
    B. a simulation
    C. a Markov model
    D. the critical path method

9. When working with members of a predominantly African-American community, specialists from other cultural backgrounds should be aware that African-Americans tend to express thoughts and feelings through descriptions of
    A. physically tangible sensations
    B. problems to be analyzed
    C. corresponding analogies
    D. spiritual issues

10. Local nonprofessionals should be considered useful to a specialist who is looking to undertake a community outreach or educational initiative.
    Which of the following is LEAST likely to be a characteristic or role demonstrated by these community members?
    A. Undertaking support functions at the agency
    B. Serving as a communication channel between the agency and clients
    C. Encouraging greater agency acceptance and credibility within the community
    D. Helping the agency to accomplish meaningful change

11. In working with Native American groups or clients, it is important to recognize that the GREATEST health problem facing their communities today is
    A. domestic violence
    B. depression and suicide
    C. alcoholism
    D. tuberculosis

12. A specialist is facilitating a cooperative conflict resolution session between community members who have different opinions about what kinds of intervention services should be offered by the local adult protective services agency.
    Which of the following is NOT a guideline that should be followed in this process?
    A. Early in the negotiations, ask each party to name the issues on which they will positively not yield.
    B. Try to get the parties to view the issue from other points of view, beside the two or three conflicting ones.
    C. Have each side volunteer what it would be willing to do to resolve the conflict.
    D. At the end of the session, draw up a formal agreement with agreed-upon actions for both parties.

13. A specialist wants to evaluate the effectiveness of a local women's shelter. The shelter has suffered from lax participation, given the number of women who have been abused in the surrounding area. The specialist wants to speak with the women in the community who did not follow up on referrals to the shelter, and begins by visiting some of these women. After gaining the trust of these women, the specialist asks for the names of women they know who might be in need of help with a domestic violence situation.
    The specialist's approach in this case is _____ sampling.
    A. maximum variation   B. snowball
    C. convenience   D. typical case

14. When it comes to perceiving messages, people typically DON'T
    A. tend to simplify causal connections and sometimes even seek a single cause to explain what may be a highly complex effect
    B. tend to perceive messages independently of a categorical framework, especially if the message may be distorted by such an interpretation
    C. have a predisposition toward accepting any pattern that a speaker offers to explain seemingly unconnected facts
    D. tend to interpret things in the way they are viewed by their reference group

15. The elder members of Native American communities, regardless of kinship, are MOST commonly referred to as
    A. the ancients   B. father or mother
    C. grandfather or grandmother D. chiefs

16. Each of the following is typically an objective of community mobilization, EXCEPT:
    A. To convince existing community resources to alter their services or work together to address an unmet need
    B. To gather and distribute information to consumers and agencies about unmet needs

C. To publicize existing community resources and make them more accessible
D. To bring an unmet community need to public attention in order to achieve acceptance of and support for fulfilling the need

17. Research in community outreach shows that women often build friendships through shared positive feelings, whereas men often build friendships through
    A. metacommunication
    B. catharsis
    C. impression management
    D. shared activities

18. Typically, the FIRST step in a community-needs assessment is to
    A. identify community's strengths
    B. explore the nature of the neighborhood
    C. get to know the area and its residents
    D. talk to people in the community

19. Most public relations experts agree that _____ exposure(s) to a message is the minimum just to get the message noticed. If the aim of a public outreach campaign is action or a change in behavior, the agency budget must plan for more exposures.
    A. one
    B. two
    C. three
    D. four

20. In the program development/community liaison model of community work and public outreach, the PRIMARY constituency is considered to be
    A. community representatives and the service agency board or administrators
    B. elected officials, social agencies, and interagency organizations
    C. marginalized or oppressed population groups in a city or region
    D. residents of a neighborhood, parish or rural county

21. Social or interpersonal problems in many African-American communities have their roots in
    A. personality deficits
    B. unresolved family conflicts
    C. poor communication
    D. external stressors

22. A public outreach campaign should
    I. focus on short-term, measurable goals, rather than ultimate outcomes
    II. try to alter entrenched attitudes within a short time, with powerfully worded messages
    III. proceed in steps or phases, each of which lays out a mechanism that leads to the desired effect
    IV. ignore causes that led to a problem, and instead focus on solutions

    The CORRECT answer is:
    A. I and II
    B. II and III
    C. III only
    D. I, II, III and IV

23. Research findings indicate that in listing preferences for helping professional attributes, individuals from culturally diverse groups are MOST likely to consider _____ as more important than _____.
    A. personality similarity; either race/ethnic similarity or attitude similarity
    B. therapist experience; any kind of similarity
    C. race/ethnic similarity; attitude similarity
    D. attitude similarity; race/ethnic similarity

24. Each of the following is considered to be an objective of community organization EXCEPT
    A. effecting changes in the distribution of decision-making power
    B. helping people develop and strengthen the traits of self-direction and cooperation
    C. effecting and maintaining the balance between needs and resources in a community
    D. helping people deal with their problems by developing alternative behaviors

25. A specialist is helping the adult protective services agency to design a public outreach campaign. The topic to be addressed is complex, public understanding is low, and most professionals at the agency feel that having more complete information might change the opinions of community members. Which method of pre-campaign research is probably MOST appropriate?
    A. Deliberative polling   B. Attitude scales
    C. Surveys or questionnaires   D. Focus groups

KEY (CORRECT ANSWERS)

1.	C	11.	C
2.	A	12.	A
3.	A	13.	B
4.	C	14.	B
5.	C	15.	C
6.	A	16.	B
7.	A	17.	D
8.	D	18.	B
9.	C	19.	C
10.	A	20.	A

21. D
22. C
23. D
24. D
25. A

TEST 2

DIRECTIONS: Each question or incomplete statement is followed by several suggested answers or completions. Select the one that BEST answers the question or completes the statement. *PRINT THE LETTER OF THE CORRECT ANSWER IN THE SPACE AT THE RIGHT.*

1. A specialist has been called in to resolve a dispute between two community leaders who have been arguing about the level of service needed within the community. The discussion has been going on for several hours when the specialist arrives, and both people seem to be upset.
After calming the two down and getting each of them to agree on a statement of the problem, the specialist should ask each person to
   A. summarize his or her argument in three main points
   B. explain why he or she became so upset
   C. clearly state, in objective terms, the position of the other in a form that meets with the other's approval
   D. identify the best alternative outcome, other than their presumed ideal

1.____

2. In evaluating the impact of a public outreach campaign, the _____ model can be used early in the campaign to address first impressions.
   A. exposure or advertising
   B. expert interview
   C. impact monitoring or process
   D. experimental or quasi-experimental

2.____

3. When trying to motivate an older population to take action on a community problem, it is helpful to remember that older people
   A. are more self-reliant in their decision-making than other members of the same family
   B. often need more time to decide than younger people
   C. are more likely than younger people to view community problems self-referentially
   D. tend to take a pragmatic, rather than philosophical, view of life

3.____

4. The method of group or community decision-making that is normally MOST time-consuming is
   A. majority opinion   B. consensus
   C. expert opinion   D. authority rule

4.____

5. A local adult protective services agency has identified one of the goals of its recent public outreach campaign to be the mobilization of activists.
The campaign should probably
   A. target neutral audiences
   B. home in on supporters
   C. stick to purely factual information
   D. try to persuade community fence-sitters

5.____

6. Research of Native American youths' perceptions of family concerns for their well-being has generally found that these youths
    A. have a high degree of uncertainty about their families' feelings toward them
    B. believe their families don't care about them
    C. believe that their mothers care a great deal about them, but their fathers don't
    D. believe their families care a great deal about them

6._____

7. A domestic violence specialist is developing a new outreach program for the local community. The specialist has defined the target problem, set program goals, and planned the actions that will take place as a result of the program. Most likely, the next step will be to
    A. evaluate the resources available to achieve program goals
    B. define and sequence the steps that will be taken to achieve program goals
    C. determine how the program will be evaluated
    D. decide how the program will operate

7._____

8. Elder: *I'm so glad to have someone to talk to, someone who really understands my problem.*
   Specialist: <u>*It is nice to be able to talk to someone who will listen.*</u>
   Elder: *That's for sure.*
   In the above exchange, what listening skill is evident in the underlined statement?
    A. Verbatim response
    B. Paraphrasing
    C. Advising
    D. Evaluation

8._____

9. Which of the following activities is involved in the specialist's task of mobilizing?
    A. Meeting individuals in the community with problems and assisting them in finding help
    B. Identifying unmet community needs
    C. Speaking out against an unjust policy or procedure
    D. Developing new services or linking presently available services to meet community needs

9._____

10. The preliminary research associated with a public outreach campaign should FIRST be aimed at determining
    A. the budget
    B. the message's ultimate audience
    C. what media to use
    D. the short-term behavioral goals of the campaign

10._____

11. A specialist in a low-income community wants to plan programs that will deal with the influence of unemployment on domestic disturbances. The specialist needs to know not only how many unemployed people are in the community now, but also how many people will be unemployed at any particular tie in the future, and how those numbers will vary given certain conditions.

11._____

Probably the BEST way to trace employment rates over time and within differing conditions is through the use of
- A. the critical path
- B. linear programming
- C. difference equations
- D. the Markov model

12. Generally, public outreach programs—whatever their stated goal—should
   I. create a sense of urgency about a problem
   II. decline to identify opponents of the issue or idea
   III. propose concrete, easily understandable solutions
   IV. urge a specific action

   The CORRECT answer is:
   - A. I only
   - B. I, III and IV
   - C. II and III
   - D. I, II, III and IV

13. Which of the following methods of community needs assessment relies to the GREATEST degree on existing public records?
   - A. Social indicators
   - B. Field study
   - C. Rates under treatment
   - D. Key informant

14. During an interview with a Native American client, a specialist is careful to maintain close and nearly constant eye contact.
   The client is MOST likely to interpret this as a(n)
   - A. show of high concern
   - B. sign of disrespect
   - C. uncomfortable assumption of intimacy
   - D. attempt to intimidate

15. The BEST strategy for addressing an audience that is known to be captive, or even hostile, is to
   - A. refer to experiences in common
   - B. flatter the audience
   - C. joke about things in or near the audience
   - D. plead for fairness

16. Integrative conflict resolution is characterized by
   - A. an overriding concern to maximize joint outcomes
   - B. one side's interests opposing the other's
   - C. a fixed and limited amount of resources to be divided, so that the more one group gets, the less another gets
   - D. manipulation and withholding information as negotiation strategies

17. A specialist wants to learn how to interact with the members of a largely Latino community in a more culturally sensitive way.
   Which of the following is NOT a guideline for interacting with members of a Latino community?
   - A. Efforts to foster independence and self-reliance may be interpreted by many Latinos as a lack of concern for others.
   - B. Efforts to deal one-on-one with an adolescent client may serve to alienate the parents, especially the mother.

C. A nonverbal gesture, such as lowering the eyes, is interpreted by many Latinos as a sign of respect and deference to authority.
D. In much of Latino culture, the focus of control for problems tends to be much more external than internal.

18. Each of the following is a supporting assumption of community organization, EXCEPT:
    A. Democracy requires cooperative participation.
    B. In order for communities to change, it is necessary for each individual in the community to be willing to change.
    C. Communities often need help with organization and planning.
    D. Holistic approaches work better than fragmented or ad-hoc programs.

18._____

19. Helping professionals often have difficulty to bring community resources together to fulfill unmet community needs.
    Which of the following is NOT usually a reason for this?
    A. Some community groups resist assistance when it is offered.
    B. Few community groups make their needs known.
    C. Community resources frequently change the type of services they offer.
    D. Often, community resources prefer to work alone.

19._____

20. When dealing with groups or populations of elderly clients, specialists should be mindful that about _____ of the nation's elderly suffer from mental health problems.
    A. a tenth   B. a quarter   C. a third   D. half

20._____

21. In an African-American community, a specialist from another culture should recognize that church participation, for most African-Americans, is viewed as a
    A. method for maintaining control and communicating competency
    B. way of depersonalizing problems or troubles
    C. way to divert attention away from problems
    D. means of cathartic emotional release

21._____

22. Adult protective service programs supported by state statutes protect elderly people from abuse and neglect under the doctrine of
    A. parens patriae   B. habeas corpus
    C. in loco parentis   D. volenti non fit injuria

22._____

23. In terms of public outreach, which of the following statements about an audience is NOT generally true?
    A. The more heterogeneous the audience, the more necessary it will be to use specific examples and appeals to certain types of people.
    B. The smaller the audience, the more likely that its members will share assumptions and values.
    C. When the speaker does not know the status of an audience, it is best to assume that they are captive rather than voluntary.
    D. The larger an audience, the more formal a presentation is likely to be.

23._____

24. A specialist often spends time in the places frequented by community residents. She listens carefully to what residents seem most concerned about, and engages many in conversations, asking them how they see the problems in the community. During these conversations, she makes mental notes about whether the statements of the problems are the same things that are mentioned in their conversations. From these conversations, the worker determines what she thinks the unmet needs of the community are.
Which of the key issues in identifying unmet needs has the worker neglected to address?
    A. The different points of view regarding the issues, and whether there is any common ground
    B. Whether the stated problems and conversations with community residents reflect the same concerns
    C. How community residents define the issues
    D. What the residents talk about with one another in a community

24.____

25. Which of the following political styles should be used to promote an issue that could become controversial if it is perceived to involve major reforms?
    A. High-conflict, polarized
    B. High-conflict, consensual
    C. Moderate conflict, compromise-oriented
    D. Low-conflict, technical

25.____

KEY (CORRECT ANSWERS)

1.	C		11.	D
2.	A		12.	B
3.	B		13.	A
4.	B		14.	B
5.	B		15.	A
6.	D		16.	A
7.	A		17.	D
8.	B		18.	B
9.	D		19.	C
10.	B		20.	B

21.	D
22.	A
23.	A
24.	A
25.	D

EXAMINATION SECTION
TEST 1

DIRECTIONS: Each question or incomplete statement is followed by several suggested answers or completions. Select the one that BEST answers the question or completes the statement. *PRINT THE LETTER OF THE CORRECT ANSWER IN THE SPACE AT THE RIGHT.*

1. Although some kinds of instructions are best put in written form, a supervisor can give many instructions verbally.
   In which one of the following situations would verbal instructions be MOST suitable?
   A. Furnishing an employee with the details to be checked in doing a certain job
   B. Instructing an employee on the changes necessary to update the office manual used in your unit
   C. Informing a new employee where different kinds of supplies and equipment that he might need are kept
   D. Presenting an assignment to an employee who will be held accountable for following a series of steps

1.____

2. You may be asked to evaluate the organization structure of your unit.
   Which one of the following questions would you NOT expect to take up in an evaluation of this kind?
   A. Is there an employee whose personal problems are interfering with his or her work?
   B. Is there an up-to-date job description for each position in this section?
   C. Are related operations and tasks grouped together and regularly assigned together?
   D. Are responsibilities divided as far as possible, and is this division clearly understood by all employees?

2.____

3. In order to distribute and schedule work fairly and efficiently, a supervisor may wish to make a work distribution study. A simple way of getting the information necessary for such a study is to have everyone for one week keep track of each task doe and the time spent on each.
   Which one of the following situations showing up in such study would MOST clearly call for corrective action?
   A. The newest employee takes longer to do most tasks than do experienced employees.
   B. One difficult operation takes longer to do than most other operations carried out by the section.
   C. A particular employee is very frequently assigned tasks that are not similar and have no relationship to each other.
   D. The most highly skilled employee is often assigned the most difficult jobs.

3.____

4. The authority to carry out a job can be delegated to a subordinate, but the supervisor remains responsible for the work of the section as a whole.
   As a supervisor, which of the following rules would be the BEST one for you to follow in view of the above statement?
   A. Avoid assigning important tasks to your subordinates, because you will be blamed if anything goes wrong
   B. Be sure each subordinate understands the specific job he has been assigned, and check at intervals to make sure assignments are done properly
   C. Assign several people to every important job so that responsibility will be spread out as much as possible
   D. Have an experienced subordinate check all work done by other employees so that there will be little chance of anything going wrong

5. The human tendency to resist change is often reflected in higher rates of turnover, absenteeism, and errors whenever an important change is made in an organization. Although psychologists do not fully understand the reasons why people resist change, they believe that the resistance stems from a threat to the individual's security, that it is a form of fear of the unknown.
   In light of this statement, which one of the following approaches would probably be MOST effective in preparing employees for a change in procedure in their unit?
   A. Avoid letting employees know anything about the change until the last possible moment
   B. Sympathize with employees who resent the change and let them know you share their doubts and fears
   C. Promise the employees that if the change turns out to be a poor one, you will allow them to suggest a return to the old system
   D. Make sure that employees know the reasons for the change and are aware of the benefits that are expected from it

6. Each of the following methods of encouraging employee participation in work planning has been used effectively with different kinds and sizes of employee groups.
   Which one of the following methods would be MOST suitable for a group of four technically skilled employees?
   A. Discussions between the supervisor and a representative of the group
   B. A suggestion program with semi-annual awards for outstanding suggestions
   C. A group discussion summoned whenever a major problem remains unsolved for more than a month
   D. Day-to-day exchange of information, opinions, and experience

7. Of the following, the MOST important reason why a supervisor is given the authority to tell subordinates what work they should do, how they should do it, and when it should be done is that usually
   A. most people will not work unless there is someone with authority standing over them

B. work is accomplished more effectively if the supervisor plans and coordinates it
C. when division of work is left up to subordinates, there is constant arguing, and very little work is accomplished
D. subordinates are not familiar with the tasks to be performed

8. Fatigue is a factor that affects productivity in all work situations. However, a brief rest period will ordinarily serve to restore a person from fatigue. According to this statement, which one of the following techniques is MOST likely to reduce the impact of fatigue on overall productivity in a unit?
   A. Scheduling several short breaks throughout the day
   B. Allowing employees to go home early
   C. Extending the lunch period an extra half hour
   D. Rotating job assignments every few weeks

9. After giving a new task to an employee, it is a good idea for a supervisor to ask specific questions to make sure that the employee grasps the essentials of the task and sees how it can be carried out. Questions which ask the employee what he thinks or how he feels about an important aspect of the task are particularly effective.
   Which one of the following questions is NOT the type of question which would be useful in the foregoing situation?
   A. Do you feel there will be any trouble meeting the 4:30 deadline?
   B. How do you feel about the kind of work we do here?
   C. Do you think that combining those two steps will work all right?
   D. Can you think of any additional equipment you may need for this process?

10. Of the following, the LEAST important reason for having a *continuous* training program is that
    A. employees may forget procedures that they have already learned
    B. employees may develop shortcuts on the job that result in inaccurate work
    C. the job continue to change because of new procedures and equipment
    D. training is one means of measuring effectiveness and productivity on the job

11. In training a new employee, it is usually advisable to break down the job into meaningful parts and have the new employee master one part before going on to the next.
    Of the following, the BEST reason for using this technique is to
    A. let the new employee know the reason for what he is doing and thus encourage him to remain in the unit
    B. make the employee aware of the importance of the work and encourage him to work harder
    C. show the employee that the work is easy so that he will be encouraged to work faster
    D. make it more likely that the employee will experience success and will be encouraged to continue learning the job

12. You may occasionally find a serious error in the work of one of your subordinates.
    Of the following, the BEST time to discuss such an error with an employee usually is
    A. immediately after the error is found
    B. after about two weeks, since you will also be able to point out some good things that the employee has accomplished
    C. when you have discovered a pattern of errors on the part of this employee so that he will not be able to dispute your criticism
    D. after the error results in a complaint by your own supervisor

12.____

13. For very important announcements to the staff, a supervisor should usually use both written and oral communications. For example, when a new procedure is to be introduced, the supervisor can more easily obtain the group's acceptance by giving his subordinates a rough draft of the new procedure and calling a meeting of all his subordinates.
    The LEAST important benefit of this technique is that it will better enable the supervisor to
    A. explain why the change is necessary
    B. make adjustments in the new procedure to meet valid staff objections
    C. assign someone to carry out the new procedure
    D. answer questions about the new procedure

13.____

14. Assume that, while you are interviewing an individual to obtain information, the individual pauses in the middle of an answer.
    The BEST of the following actions for you to take at that time is to
    A. correct any inaccuracies in what he has said
    B. remain silent until he continues
    C. explain your position on the matter being discussed
    D. explain that time is short and that he must complete his story quickly

14.____

15. When you are interviewing someone to obtain information, the BEST of the following reasons for you to repeat certain of his exact words is to
    A. assure him that appropriate action will be taken
    B. encourage him to switch to another topic of discussion
    C. assure him that you agree with his point of view
    D. encourage him to elaborate on a point he has made

15.____

16. Generally, when writing a letter, the use of precise words and concise sentences is
    A. *good*, because less time will be required to write the letter
    B. *bad*, because it is most likely that the reader will think the letter is unimportant and will not respond favorably
    C. *good*, because it is likely that your desired meaning will be conveyed to the reader
    D. *bad*, because your letter will be too brief to provide adequate information

16.____

17. In which of the following cases would it be MOST desirable to have two cards for one individual in a single alphabetic file?
The individual has
    A. a hyphenated surname
    B. two middle names
    C. a first name with an unusual spelling
    D. a compound first name

17.____

18. Of the following, it is MOST appropriate to use a form letter when it is necessary to answer many
    A. requests or inquiries from a single individual
    B. follow-up letters from individuals requesting additional information
    C. request or inquiries about a single subject
    D. complaints from individuals that they have been unable to obtain various types of information

18.____

19. Assume that you are asked to make up a budget for your section for the coming year, and you are told that the most important function of the budget is its "control function."
Of the following, "control" in this context implies MOST NEARLY that
    A. you will probably be asked to justify expenditures in any category when it looks as though these expenditures are departing greatly from the amount budgeted
    B. your section will probably not be allowed to spend more than the budgeted amount in any given category, although it is always permissible to spend less
    C. your section will be required to spend the exact amount budgeted in every category
    D. the budget will be filed in the Office of the Comptroller so that when a year is over the actual expenditures can be compared with the amounts in the budget

19.____

20. In writing a report, the practice of taking up the LEAST important points *first* and the most important points *last* is a
    A. *good* technique, since the final points made in a report will make the greatest impression on the reader
    B. *good* technique, since the material is presented in a more logical manner and will lead directly to the conclusions
    C. *poor* technique, since the reader's time is wasted by having to review irrelevant information before finishing the report
    D. *poor* technique, since it may cause the reader to lose interest in the report and arrive at incorrect conclusions about the report

20.____

21. Typically, when the technique of "supervision by results" is practiced, higher management sets down, either implicitly or explicitly, certain performance standards or goals that the subordinate is expected to meet. So long as these standards are met, management interferes very little.
The MOST likely result of the use of this technique is that it will

21.____

A. lead to ambiguity in terms of goals
B. be successful only to the extent that close direct supervision is practiced
C. make it possible to evaluate both employee and supervisory effectiveness
D. allow for complete dependence on the subordinate's part

22. When making written evaluations and reviews of the performance of subordinates, it is usually ADVISABLE to
    A. avoid informing the employee of the evaluation if it is critical because it may create hard feelings
    B. avoid informing the employee of the evaluation whether critical or favorable because it is tension-producing
    C. to permit the employee to see the evaluation but not to discuss it with him because the supervisor cannot be certain where the discussion might lead
    D. to discuss the evaluation openly with the employee because it helps the employee understand what is expected of him

23. There are a number of well-known and respected human relations principles that successful supervisors have been using for years in building good relationships with their employees.
    Which of the following does NOT illustrate such a principle?
    A. Give clear and complete instructions
    B. Let each person know how he is getting along
    C. Keep an open-door policy
    D. Make all relationships personal ones

24. Assume that it is necessary for you to give an unpleasant assignment to one of your subordinates. You expect this employee to raise some objections to this assignment.
    The MOST appropriate of the following actions for you to take FIRST is to issue the assignment
    A. *orally*, with the further statement that you will not listen to any complaints
    B. *in writing*, to forestall any complaints by the employee
    C. *orally*, permitting the employee to express his feelings
    D. *in writing*, with a note that any comments should be submitted in writing

25. Suppose you have just announced at a staff meeting with your subordinates that a radical reorganization of work will take place next week. Your subordinates at the meeting appear to be excited, tense, and worried.
    Of the following, the BEST action for you to take at that time is to
    A. schedule private conferences with each subordinate to obtain his reaction to the meeting
    B. close the meeting and tell your subordinates to return immediately to their work assignments
    C. give your subordinates some time to ask questions and discuss your announcement
    D. insist that your subordinates do not discuss your announcement among themselves or with other members of the agency

KEY (CORRECT ANSWERS)

1.	C		11.	D
2.	A		12.	A
3.	C		13.	C
4.	B		14.	B
5.	D		15.	D
6.	D		16.	C
7.	B		17.	A
8.	A		18.	C
9.	B		19.	A
10.	D		20.	D

21. C
22. D
23. D
24. C
25. C

TEST 2

DIRECTIONS: Each question or incomplete statement is followed by several suggested answers or completions. Select the one that BEST answers the question or completes the statement. *PRINT THE LETTER OF THE CORRECT ANSWER IN THE SPACE AT THE RIGHT.*

1. Of the following, the BEST way for a supervisor to increase employees' interest in their work is to
    A. allow them to make as many decisions as possible
    B. demonstrate to them that he is as technically competent as they
    C. give each employee a difficult assignment
    D. promptly convey to them instructions from higher management

    1.____

2. The one of the following which is LEAST important in maintaining a high level of productivity on the part of employees is the
    A. provision of optimum physical working conditions for employees
    B. strength of employees' aspirations for promotion
    C. anticipated satisfactions which employees hope to derive from their work
    D. employees' interest in their jobs

    2.____

3. Of the following, the MAJOR advantage of group problem-solving, as compared to individual problem-solving, is that groups will more readily
    A. abide by their own decisions
    B. agree with agency management
    C. devise new policies and procedures
    D. reach conclusions sooner

    3.____

4. The group problem-solving conference is a useful supervisory method for getting people to reach solutions to problems.
    Of the following, the reason that groups usually reach more realistic solutions than do individuals is that
    A. individuals, as a rule, take longer than do groups in reaching decisions and are, therefore, more likely to make an error
    B. bringing people together to let them confer impresses participants with the seriousness of problems
    C. groups are generally more concerned with the future in evaluating organizational problems
    D. the erroneous opinions of group members tend to be corrected by the other members

    4.____

5. A competent supervisor should be able to distinguish between human and technical problems.
    Of the following, the MAJOR difference between such problems is that serious human problems, in comparison to ordinary technical problems
    A. are remedied more quickly
    B. involve a lesser need for diagnosis
    C. are more difficult to define
    D. become known through indications which are usually the actual problem

    5.____

6. Of the following, the BEST justification for a public agency establishing an alcoholism program for its employees is that
   A. alcoholism has traditionally been looked upon with a certain amused tolerance by management and thereby ignored as a serious illness
   B. employees with drinking problems have twice as many on-the-job accidents, especially during the early years of the problem
   C. excessive use of alcohol is associated with personality instability hindering informal social relationships among peers and subordinates
   D. the agency's public reputation will suffer despite an employee's drinking problem being a personal matter of little public concern

7. Assume you are a manager and you find a group of maintenance employees assigned to your project drinking and playing cards for money in an incinerator room after their regular working hours.
   The one of the following actions it would be BEST for you to take is to
   A. suspend all employees immediately if there is no question in your mind as to the validity of the charges
   B. review the personnel records of those involved with the supervisor and make a joint decision on which employees should sustain penalties of loss of annual leave or fines
   C. ask the supervisor to interview each violator and submit written reports to you and thereafter consult with the supervisor about disciplinary actions
   D. deduct three days of annual leave from each employee involved if he pleads guilty in lieu of facing more serious charges

8. Assume that as a manager you must discipline a subordinate, but all of the pertinent facts necessary for a full determination of the appropriate action to take are not yet available. However, you fear that a delay in disciplinary action may damage the morale of other employees.
   The one of the following which is MOST appropriate for you to do in this matter is to
   A. take immediate disciplinary action as if all the pertinent facts were available
   B. wait until all pertinent facts are available before reaching a decision
   C. inform the subordinate that you know he is guilty, issue a stern warning, and then let him wait for your further action
   D. reduce the severity of the discipline appropriate for the violation

9. There are two standard dismissal procedures utilized by most public agencies. The first is the "open back door" policy, in which the decision of a supervisor in discharging an employee for reasons of inefficiency cannot be cancelled by the central personnel agency. The second is the "closed back door" policy, in which the central personnel agency can order the supervisor to restore the discharged employee to his position.
   Of the following, the major DISADVANTAGE of the "closed back door" policy as opposed to the "open back door" policy is that central personnel agencies are
   A. likely to approve the dismissal of employees when there is inadequate justification

    B. likely to revoke dismissal actions out of sympathy for employees
    C. less qualified than employing agencies to evaluate the efficiency of employees
    D. easily influenced by political, religious, and racial factors

10. The one of the following for which a formal grievance-handling system is LEAST useful is in   10.____
    A. reducing the frequency of employee complaints
    B. diminishing the likelihood of arbitrary action by supervisors
    C. providing an outlet for employee frustrations
    D. bringing employee problems to the attention of higher management

11. The one of the following managers whose leadership style involves the GREATEST delegation of authority to subordinates is the one who presents to subordinates   11.____
    A. his ideas and invites questions
    B. his decision and persuades them to accept it
    C. the problem, gets their suggestions, and makes his decision
    D. a tentative decision which is subject to change

12. Which of the following is MOST likely to cause employee productivity standards to be set too high?   12.____
    A. Standards of productivity are set by first-line supervisors rather than by higher level managers.
    B. Employees' opinions about productivity standards are sought through written questionnaires.
    C. Initial studies concerning productivity are conducted by staff specialists.
    D. Ideal work conditions assumed in the productivity standards are lacking in actual operations.

13. The one of the following which states the MAIN value of an organization chart for a manager is that such charts show the   13.____
    A. lines of formal authority
    B. manner in which duties are performed by each employee
    C. flow of work among employees on the same level
    D. specific responsibilities of each position

14. Which of the following BEST names the usual role of a line unit with regard to the organization's programs?   14.____
    A. Seeking publicity   B. Developing
    C. Carrying out   D. Evaluating

15. Critics of promotion *from within* a public agency argue for hiring *from outside* the agency because they believe that promotion from within leads to   15.____
    A. resentment and consequent weakened morale on the part of those not promoted
    B. the perpetuation of outdated practices and policies
    C. a more complex hiring procedure than hiring from outside the agency
    D. problems of objectively appraising someone already in the organization

16. The one of the following management functions which usually can be handled MOST effectively by a committee is the
    A. settlement of interdepartmental disputes
    B. planning of routine work schedules
    C. dissemination of information
    D. assignment of personnel

17. Assume that you are serving on a committee which is considering proposals in order to recommend a new maintenance policy. After eliminating a number of proposals by unanimous consent, the committee is deadlocked on three proposals.
    The one of the following which is the BEST way for the committee to reach agreement on a proposal they could recommend is to
    A. consider and vote on each proposal separately by secret ballot
    B. examine and discuss the three proposals until the proponents of two of them are persuaded they are wrong
    C. reach a synthesis which incorporates the significant features of each proposals
    D. discuss the three proposals until the proponents of each one concede those aspects of the proposals about which there is disagreement

18. A commonly used training and development method for professional staff is the case method, which utilizes the description of a situation, real or simulated, to provide a common base for analysis, discussion, and problem-solving.
    Of the following, the MOST appropriate time to use the case method is when professional staff needs
    A. insight into their personality problems
    B. practice in applying management concepts to their own problems
    C. practical experience in the assignment of delegated responsibilities
    D. to know how to function in many different capacities

19. The incident process is a training and development method in which trainees are given a very brief statement of an event or o a situation presenting a job incident or an employee problem of special significance.
    Of the following, it is MOST appropriate to use the incident process when
    A. trainees need to learn to review and analyze facts before solving a problem
    B. there are a large number of trainees who require the same information
    C. there are too many trainees to carry on effective discussion
    D. trainees are not aware of the effect of their behavior on others

20. The one of the following types of information about which a clerical employee is usually LEAST concerned during the orientation process is
    A. his specific job duties   B. where he will work
    C. his organization's history   D. who his associates will be

21. The one of the following which is the MOST important limitation on the degree to which work should be broken down into specialized tasks is the point at which
    A. there ceases to be sufficient work of a specialized nature to occupy employees
    B. training costs equal the half-yearly savings derived from further specialization
    C. supervision of employees performing specialized tasks becomes more technical than supervision of general employees
    D. it becomes more difficult to replace the specialist than to replace the generalist who performs a complex set of functions

22. When a supervisor is asked for his opinion of the suitability for promotion of a subordinate, the supervisor is actually being asked to predict the subordinate's future behavior in a new role.
    Such a prediction is MOST likely to be accurate if the
    A. higher position is similar to the subordinate's current one
    B. higher position requires intangible personal qualities
    C. new position has had little personal association with the subordinate away from the job

23. In one form of the non-directive evaluation interview, the supervisor communicates his evaluation to the employee and then listens to the employee's response without making further suggestions.
    The one of the following which is the PRINCIPAL danger of this method of evaluation is that the employee is MOST likely to
    A. develop an indifferent attitude towards the supervisor
    B. fail to discover ways of improving his performance
    C. become resistant to change in the organization's structure
    D. place the blame for his shortcomings on his co-workers

24. In establishing rules for his subordinates, a superior should be PRIMARILY concerned with
    A. creating sufficient flexibility to allow for exceptions
    B. making employees aware of the reasons for the rules and the penalties for infractions
    C. establishing the strength of his own position in relation to his subordinates
    D. having his subordinates know that such rules will be imposed in a personal manner

25. The practice of conducting staff training sessions on a periodic basis is generally considered
    A. *poor*; it takes employees away from their work assignments
    B. *poor*; all staff training should be done on an individual basis
    C. *good*; it permits the regular introduction of new methods and techniques
    D. *good*; it ensures a high employee productivity rate

KEY (CORRECT ANSWERS)

1.	A	11.	C
2.	A	12.	D
3.	A	13.	A
4.	D	14.	C
5.	C	15.	B
6.	B	16.	A
7.	C	17.	C
8.	B	18.	B
9.	C	19.	A
10.	A	20.	C

21.	A
22.	A
23.	B
24.	B
25.	C

EXAMINATION SECTION
TEST 1

DIRECTIONS: Each question or incomplete statement is followed by several suggested answers or completions. Select the one that BEST answers the question or completes the statement. *PRINT THE LETTER OF THE CORRECT ANSWER IN THE SPACE AT THE RIGHT.*

1. The MAJOR responsibility of a director is to
   A. make certain that his line supervisors keep proper control of staff activity
   B. see that training is given to his staff according to individual needs
   C. insure that his total organization is coordinated toward agency goals and objectives
   D. work constructively with groups so that programs will reflect their needs

   1.____

2. A good organizational chart of a department is an IMPORTANT instrument because it can
   A. make it easier to understand the mission of the department
   B. help new employees become acquainted with department personnel
   C. clarify relationships and responsibilities of the various department components
   D. simplify the task of *going to the top*

   2.____

3. Unnecessary and obsolete forms can be eliminated MOST effectively by
   A. appointing a representative committee to review and evaluate all forms in relation to operating procedures
   B. discarding all forms which have not been used during the past year
   C. assembling all forms and destroying those which are duplicates or obsolete
   D. directing office managers to review the forms to determine which should be revised or abolished

   3.____

4. The director must adopt methods and techniques to insure that his budgeted allowances are properly spent and that organizational objectives are being reached.
   These responsibilities can be fulfilled BEST by
   A. controlling operations with electronic data processing equipment
   B. shifting caseload controls from caseworkers to clerical staff
   C. installing a work simplification program and establishing controls for crucial areas of operation
   D. assigning employees with special skills and training to perform the more important and specialized jobs

   4.____

5. The MOST appropriate technique for making the staff thoroughly familiar with department policies would be to
   A. maintain an up-to-date loose-leaf binder of written policies in a central point in the office
   B. issue copies of all policy directives to the unit supervisors
   C. distribute copies of policy directives to the entire staff and arrange for follow-up discussion on a unit basis
   D. discuss all major policy directives at an office-wide staff meeting

6. When a proposed change in a departmental procedure is being evaluated, the factor which should be considered MOST important in reaching the decision is the
   A. extent of resistance anticipated from members of the staff
   B. personnel needed to execute the proposed change
   C. time required for training staff in the revised procedure
   D. degree of organizational dislocation compared with gains expected from the change

7. A director anticipates that certain aspects of a new departmental procedure will be distasteful to many staff members.
   Assuming that the procedure is basically sound in spite of this drawback, the BEST approach for the director to take with his staff is to
   A. advise them to accept the procedure since it has the support of the highest authorities in the department
   B. point out that other procedures which were resisted initially have come to be accepted in time
   C. challenge staff members to suggest another procedure which will accomplish the same purpose better
   D. ask the staff members to discuss the *pros* and *cons* of the procedure and suggest how it can be improved

8. At a staff meeting at which a basic change in departmental procedure is to be announced, a director begins the discussion by asking the participants for criticisms of the existing procedure. He then describes the new procedure to be employed and explains the improvements that are anticipated.
   The director's method of introducing the change is
   A. *good*, mainly because the participants would be more receptive to the new procedure is they understood the inadequacies of the old one
   B. *good*, mainly because the participants' comments on the old procedure will provide the basis for evaluation of the feasibility of the new one
   C. *bad*, mainly because the participants will realize that the decision for change has been made before the meeting, without consideration of the participants' comments
   D. *bad*, mainly because the discussion is focused on the old procedure, rather than on the procedure being introduced

9. Assume that you are conducting a staff conference to discuss the development of a procedure implementing a change in state policy. There are twelve participants whose office titles range from unit supervisor to senior supervisor, each of whom has responsibility for some aspect of the program affected by the policy change.
After some introductory remarks, the BEST procedure for you to follow is to call upon the participants in the order of their
    A. titles, with the highest titles first because they are likely to have the most experience and knowledge of the subject
    B. titles, with the lower titles first because they are likely to be less inhibited if they are permitted to give their views before the senior participants speak
    C. places around the table, to promote informality and democratic procedure
    D. specialized knowledge of the subject so that those with the most knowledge and competence may lead the discussion

9.____

10. A staff member has suggested a way of reducing the time required to prepare a monthly report by combining several items of information, separating one item into two part, and generally revising definitions of terms.
The CHIEF disadvantage of such a revision is that
    A. comparison of present with past periods will be more difficult
    B. subordinates who prepare the report will require retraining
    C. forms currently in use will have to be discarded
    D. employees using the records will be confused by the changes

10.____

11. Assume that a director happens to be present at a regular staff conference conducted by a senior supervisor. During the course of the conference, the director frequently takes over the discussion in order to amplify remarks made by the supervisor, to impart information about departmental policies, and to modify or correct possible misinterpretations of the supervisor's remarks.
The director's actions in this situation are
    A. *proper*, mainly because the conference members were given the latest and most accurate information concerning departmental policies
    B. *proper*, mainly because the director has an obligation to assist and support the supervisor
    C. *improper*, mainly because the director did not completely take over the conference
    D. *improper*, mainly because the supervisor was put in a difficult position in the presence of his staff

11.____

12. A center has a serious staff morale problem because of rumors that it will probably be abolished. To handle this situation, the direct adopts a policy of promptly corroborating rumors that he knows to be true and denying false ones.
Although this method of dealing with the situation should have some good results, its CHIEF weakness is that
    A. it chases the rumors instead of forestalling them by giving correct information concerning the center's future

12.____

B. the director may not have the necessary information at hand
C. status is given to the rumors as a result of the attention paid to them
D. the director may inadvertently divulge confidential information

13. Realizing the importance of harmonious staff relationships, one of your supervisors makes a practice of unobtrusively intervening in any conflict situation among staff members. Whenever friction seems to be developing, he attempts to soothe ruffled feelings and remove the source of difficulty by such methods as rescheduling, reassigning personnel, etc. His efforts are always behind the scenes and unknown to the personnel involved.
This practice may produce some good results, but the CHIEF drawback is that it
    A. permits staff to engage in unacceptable practices without correction
    B. violates the principle of chain of command
    C. involves the supervisor in personal relationships which are not properly his concern
    D. requires confidential sources of information about personal relationships within the center

14. Assume that the department adopts a policy of transferring administrative personnel from one center to another after stated periods of service in a center, or in a central office.
Of the following, the MAIN advantage of such a policy is that it helps
    A. prevent the formation of cliques among staff members
    B. key staff members keep abreast of new developments
    C. effect a greater utilization of staff members' special talents
    D. develop a broader outlook and loyalty to the department as a whole, rather than to one center

15. A delegation of union members meets with you in your role as director to discuss obtaining assistance for a group of strikers who live in the neighborhood covered by the center. In the course of discussion, you learn that the strike has been called by the local union against the explicit directive of the national union's leadership.
The MOST appropriate course of action for you to take in this instance is to advise the union committee
    A. of your sympathy and assure them that individual applications from the strikers for assistance will receive priority
    B. that if the strikers are in need, they will be able to receive assistance as long as they are on strike
    C. that since the strike is illegal, none of the workers will be eligible for assistance
    D. that there is no bar to an of the strikers receiving assistance provided they are in need and are ready and willing to accept other employment if offered

16. The quality control system is a management tool used to test the validity of the eligibility caseload.
This system can be helpful to a director in the following ways, with the EXCEPTION of
    A. obtaining objective data to use in evaluating the performance of specific staff members
    B. identifying the need for policy changes
    C. sorting out the source of errors in determining eligibility
    D. setting up training objectives for his staff

17. As director, you observe that there has been a sharp rise in the number of fair hearings. The increase seems to coincide with the intensified activities of the local recipients' organization.
The MOST appropriate action under the circumstances is to
    A. determine whether the fair hearing requests result from weaknesses in the center's operation, and remedy the causes, if feasible
    B. disregard the matter for the time being because complaints have been stirred up by an organized client group
    C. emphasize to your staff the importance of meeting client needs promptly in order to avoid fair hearing requests
    D. resolve the grievances with the leaders of the recipients' organization

18. As director, you receive notice of a fair hearing decision from the State Commissioner ordering you to restore assistance to a family. You are appalled by the order because the facts cited by the hearing officer are at complete variance with what actually occurred, according to your personal knowledge of the case.
Of the following, the MOST appropriate course of action for you to take FIRST is to
    A. point out to central office that the decision should be reconsidered and appropriately modified
    B. comply with the decision under protest because it is patently wrong
    C. recommend to central office that it consider court action through an Article 78 proceeding to correct the erroneous decision
    D. comply with the decision, although an order of the State Commissioner has no force and effect of law

19. In your capacity as director, you have received a copy of the monthly statistical report issued by the department. In reviewing the report, you note that your center is showing a rise in caseload which is substantially higher than the average rise throughout the city.
Which of the alternatives listed below would be MOST appropriate in order to deal with this situation?
    A. Make plans to discuss the situation with central office so that appropriate corrective action can be taken on the basis of your consultation
    B. Collect necessary information and data about the operations of your center and the area it serves to determine the cause of the trend, and plan appropriate action on the basis of your findings

C. Call a meeting of your unit supervisors in order to impress upon them the importance of more diligent efforts to assist clients
D. Assume that the rise in caseload is an inevitable result of the substantial increase in unemployment, and take no immediate action

20. Of the following phases of a training program for administrative personnel, the one which is usually the MOST difficult to formulate is the
    A. selection of training methods for the program
    B. obtaining of frank opinions of the participants as to the usefulness of the program
    C. chief executive officer's judgment as to the need for such a program
    D. evaluation of the effectiveness of the program

21. Assume that you are conducting a conference dealing with problems of the center of which you are the director. The problem being discussed is one with which you have had no experience. However, two of the participants, who have had considerable experience with it, carry on an extended discussion, showing that they understand the problem thoroughly. The others are very much interested in the discussion and are taking notes on the material presented.
    To permit the two staff members to continue for the length of time allowed for discussion of the problem is
    A. *desirable*, chiefly because introduction of the material by the two participants themselves may encourage others to contribute their work experience
    B. *desirable*, chiefly because their discussion may be more meaningful to the others than a discussion which is not based on work experience
    C. *undesirable*, chiefly because they are discussing material only in light of their own experience rather than in general terms
    D. *undesirable*, chiefly because it would reveal your own lack of experience with the problem and undermine your authority with the staff

22. In dealing with staff members, it is a commonly accepted principle that individual differences exist, suggesting that employees should be treated in an unlike manner in order to achieve maximum results from their work assignments.
    This statement means MOST NEARLY that
    A. supervisors should be aware of the personal problems of their subordinates and make allowances for poor performance because of such problems
    B. standardized work rules are ineffective because of the different capabilities of employees to maintain such work rules
    C. employees' individual needs should be considered by their supervisors to the greatest extent possible, within the practical limitations of the work situation
    D. knowledge of general principles of human behavior is generally of little use to a supervisor in assisting him to supervise his subordinates effectively

23. A supervisor under your jurisdiction reports to you that one of his subordinates has been taking unusually long lunch hours, has been absent from work frequently, and has been doing poorer work than previously.
   The BEST procedure for you to follow FIRST is to advise the supervisor to
   A. prefer charges against the employee
   B. arrange for a psychological consultation for the employee
   C. ascertain whether the employee is ill and, if so, arrange a medical examination for him
   D. have a private conversation with the employee to obtain more information about the reasons for his behavior

23.____

24. If the term *executive development* is defined as the continuous, ongoing, on-the-job process of constructing plans to improve individuals in specific positions, both for the purpose of present improvement as well as for any future advancement which is envisaged for the employee, it follows that the emphasis in an executive development program should
   A. provide learning experiences through formal or informal classes, seminars, or conferences, for which the focus is on the function of the position
   B. be oriented to the individual participant and may include a host of planned activities, such as appraisal, coaching, counseling, and job rotation
   C. attempt to create needs, to awaken, enlarge, and stimulate the individual so as to broaden his outlook and potentialities as a human being
   D. insure that the individual is able to plan, organize, direct, and control operations in the bureau, division, or agency

24.____

25. Most psychologists agree that employees have a need for recognition for the work they perform.
   Therefore, it can be concluded that
   A. employees should be praised every time they complete a job satisfactorily
   B. praise is a more effective incentive to good performance than is punishment
   C. administrative personnel should be aware that subordinates do not have needs similar to their own
   D. a formalized system of rewards and punishment is better than no system at all, as long as there is a built-in consistency in its administration

25.____

KEY (CORRECT ANSWERS)

1.	C	11.	D
2.	C	12.	A
3.	A	13.	A
4.	C	14.	D
5.	C	15.	D
6.	D	16.	A
7.	D	17.	A
8.	C	18.	A
9.	D	19.	B
10.	A	20.	D

21. B
22. C
23. D
24. B
25. B

TEST 2

DIRECTIONS: Each question or incomplete statement is followed by several suggested answers or completions. Select the one that BEST answers the question or completes the statement. *PRINT THE LETTER OF THE CORRECT ANSWER IN THE SPACE AT THE RIGHT.*

1. Studies have shown that the MOST effective kind of safety training program is one in which the
   A. training is conducted by consultants who are expert in the nature of the work performed
   B. lectures are given by the top executives in an agency
   C. employees participate in all phases of the program
   D. supervisors are responsible for the safety training

   1._____

2. Of the following, the MOST effective method of selecting potential top executives would be
   A. situational testing which simulates actual conditions
   B. a written test which covers the knowledge required to perform the job
   C. an oral test which requires candidate to discuss significant aspects of the job
   D. a confidential interview with his former employee

   2._____

3. With regard to staff morale, MOST evidence shows that
   A. employees with positive job attitudes always outproduce those with negative job attitudes
   B. morale always relates to the employee's attitude toward his working conditions and his job
   C. low morale always results in poor job performance
   D. high morale has a direct relationship to effective union leadership

   3._____

4. Of the following groups of factors, the group which has been shown to be related to the incidence of job accidents is
   A. personality characteristics, intelligence, defective vision
   B. experience, fatigue, motor and perceptual speed
   C. coordination, fatigue, intelligence
   D. defective vision, motor and perceptual speed, intelligence

   4._____

5. Executives who have difficulty making decisions when faced with a number of choices USUALLY
   A. have domestic problems which interfere with the decision-making process
   B. can be trained to improve their ability to make decisions
   C. are production-oriented rather than employee-centered
   D. do not know their jobs well enough to act decisively

   5._____

6. Studies of disciplinary dismissals of workers reveal that
   A. the majority of employees were dismissed because of lack of technical competence
   B. the supervisors were unusually demanding of employee competence
   C. most employees were dismissed because of inability to work with their co-workers
   D. the chief executive set unrealistic standards of performance

7. One philosophy of assigning workers to a specific job is that the worker and his job are an integral unit.
   This means MOST NEARLY that the
   A. employee and the job may both require adjustment
   B. employee must meet all the specifications of the job as a prerequisite for employment
   C. employee's morale will be affected by his salary
   D. employee's job satisfaction has a direct effect on his emotional health

8. The statement that the supervisor and the administrator are the *primary personnel men* means MOST NEARLY that
   A. supervisors and administrators are more skilled in personnel techniques than are professional personnel technicians
   B. they are in the best position to implement personnel policies and procedures
   C. employees have more confidence in their supervisors and administrators than in the professional personnel administrator
   D. personnel administration is most effective when it combines both centralized and decentralized approaches

9. Administrators frequently have to interview people in order to obtain information. Although the interview is a legitimate fact-gathering technique, it has limitations which should not be overlooked.
   The one of the following which is an IMPORTANT limitation is that
   A. individuals generally hesitate to give information orally which they would usually answer in writing
   B. the material derived from the interview can usually be obtained at lower cost from existing records
   C. the emotional attitudes of individuals during an interview often affect the accuracy of the information given
   D. the interview is a poor technique for discovering how well clients understand departmental policies

10. Leadership styles have frequently been categorized as authoritarian, laissez-faire, and democratic.
    In general, management's reliance on leadership to produce desired results would be MOST effectively implemented through
    A. the laissez-faire approach when group results are desired
    B. the authoritarian approach in a benevolent manner when quick decisions are required

C. the democratic approach, when quick decisions are unimportant
D. all three approaches, depending upon circumstances

11. As director, you are responsible for enforcing a recently established regulation which has aroused antagonism among many clients.
You should deal with this situation by
    A. explaining to the clients that you are not responsible for making regulations
    B. enforcing the regulation but reporting to your superior the number and kind of complaints against it
    C. carrying out your duty of enforcing the regulation as well as you can without comment
    D. suggesting to your clients that you may overlook violations of the regulation

11.____

12. One of the observations made in a recent psychological study of leadership is that the behavior of a new employee in a leadership position can be predicted more accurately on the basis of the behavior of the previous incumbent in the post than on the behavior of the new employee in his previous job.
The BEST explanation for this observation is that there is a tendency
    A. for a newly appointed executive to avoid making basic changes in operational procedures
    B. to choose similar types of personalities to fill the same type of position
    C. for a given organizational structure and set of duties and responsibilities to produce similar patterns of behavior
    D. for executives to develop more mature patterns of behavior as a result of increased responsibility

12.____

13. A director finds that reports submitted by him to his subordinates tend to emphasize the favorable and minimize the unfavorable aspects of situations.
The MOST valid reason for this is that
    A. subordinates usually hesitate to give their supervisors an honest picture of a situation
    B. the director may not have been sufficiently critical of previous reports submitted by his subordinates
    C. subordinates have a normal tendency to represent themselves and their actions in the best possible light
    D. many subordinates in the field have developed a tendency to understatement in the depiction of unfavorable situations

13.____

14. Effective delegation of authority and responsibility to subordinates is essential for the proper administration of a center. However, the director should retain some activities under his direct control.
Of the following activities, the one for which there is LEAST justification for delegation by the director to a subordinate is one involving
    A. relationships with client groups
    B. physical danger to clients
    C. policies which are unpopular with staff
    D. matters for which there are no established policies

14.____

15. According to the principle of *span of control*, there should be a limited number of subordinates reporting to one supervisor.
Of the following, the CHIEF disadvantage which may result from the application of this principle is a reduction in the
    A. contact between lower ranking staff members and higher ranking administrative personnel
    B. freedom of action of subordinates
    C. authority and responsibility of subordinates
    D. number of organizational levels through which a matter must pass before action is taken

15.____

16. The CHIEF objection to a practice of decentralizing the preparation and distribution of memoranda by bureaus, rather than controlling distribution through central office is that it is LIKELY to result in
    A. overloading bureaus with a multiplicity of communications
    B. limited and specialized rather than broad and general viewpoints in the memoranda
    C. violation of the principle of unit of command
    D. unimportant information being communicated to all bureaus

16.____

17. A report has been completed by members of your staff. As director, you have reviewed the report and feel that the information revealed could be damaging to the department. You find yourself in conflict in your multiple role as director, as a professional, and as a citizen.
The one of the following actions which would be MOST desirable for you to take FIRST would be to
    A. send a copy of the report to your supervisor and request an immediate conference with him
    B. instruct staff to re-check the report and defer issuance of the report until the findings are confirmed
    C. immediately share the report with your supervisors and your advisory committee
    D. file the report until your advisory committee makes a request for it

17.____

18. In order for employees to function effectively, they should have a feeling of being treated fairly by management.
Which of the following general policies is MOST likely to give employees such a feeling?
    A. An employee publication should be mailed directly to the home of each employee.
    B. Employee attitude surveys should be conducted at regular intervals.
    C. Employees should be consulted and kept informed on all matters that affect them.
    D. Employees should be informed when the press publishes statements of policy.

18.____

19. In order to give employees greater job satisfaction, some management experts advocate a policy of job enrichment.
The one of the following which would be the BEST example of job enrichment is to
    A. allow an aide to decide which portion of his normal duties and responsibilities he prefers
    B. increase the fringe benefits currently available to paraprofessional employees
    C. add variety to the duties of an employee
    D. permit more flexible working schedules for professional employees

19.____

20. Management of large organizations has often emphasized high salaries and fringe benefits as the most important means of motivating employees.
The one of the following which is NOT an argument used to support this approach is
    A. most people endure work mainly in order to collect the rewards and to have the opportunity to enjoy them
    B. material incentives have proved to be the best means of stimulating creative capacity and the will to work
    C. the majority of employees place little emphasis on work-centered motivation to perform
    D. numerous research studies have shown that pay ranks first on a scale of factors motivating employees in government and industry in the United States

20.____

21. Some organizations provide psychologists or other professionally trained persons with whom employees can consult on a confidential basis regarding personal problems.
Of the following, which is MOST likely to be a benefit management can derive from such a practice?
    A. Increase in the authority of management
    B. Disclosure of the corrupt practices of those handling money
    C. Receipt of new ideas and approaches to organizational problems
    D. Obtaining tighter control on employees' private behavior

21.____

22. Authorities agree that it is generally most desirable for an employee experiencing mental health problems to seek competent professional help without being required or forced to do so by another person.
They view self-referral as a most desirable action PRIMARILY because
    A. it shows that the employee probably is more aware of the problem and more highly motivated to solve his problems
    B. the employee's right to privacy in his personal affairs is maintained
    C. another person cannot be blamed in the event the outcome of the referral is not successful
    D. the employee knows best his problems and will do what is necessary to serve his own best interests

22.____

Questions 23-25.

DIRECTIONS: Questions 23 through 25 consist of three excerpts each. Consider an excerpt correct if all the statements in the excerpt are correct. Mark your answer as follows:
A. if only excerpts I and II are correct
B. if only excerpts II and III are correct
C. if only excerpt I is correct
D. if only excerpt II is correct

23. I. Many executive decisions are based on assumptions. They may be assumptions supported by sketchy data about future needs for services; assumptions about the attitudes and future behavior of employees, perhaps based on reports of staff members or hearsay evidence; or assumptions about agency values that are as much a reflection of personal desires as of agency goals.
    II. A good pattern of well-conceived plans is only a first step in administration. The administrator must also create an organization to formulate and carry out such plans. Resources must be assembled; supervision of actual operations is necessary; and before the executive's task is completed, he must exercise control.
    III. When a problem is well defined, good alternatives identified, and the likely consequences of each alternative forecast as best we can, one can assume that the final choice of action to be taken would be easy, if not obvious.

23.____

24. I. Principles of motivation are not difficult to establish because human behavior is not complex and is easily understood; individual differences in human beings are substantial; and people are continuously learning and changing.
    II. What gives employees satisfaction or dissatisfaction indicates the nature of the motivation problem and provides positive guidance to the administrator who faces the problem of trying to get people to carry out a set of plans.
    III. The administrator's job of motivation can be described as that of creating a situation in which actions that provide net satisfaction to individual members of the enterprise are at the same time actions that make appropriate contributions toward the objectives of the enterprise.

24.____

25. I. Administrative organization is primarily concerned with legal, technical, or ultimate authority; the operational authority relationships that may be created by organization are of major significance.
    II. Accountability is not removed by delegation. Appraisal of results should be tempered by the extent to which an administrator must rely on subordinates.
    III. In delegations to operating subordinate, authority to plan exceeds authority to do, inasmuch as the executive typically reserves some of the planning for himself.

25.____

7 (#2)

KEY (CORRECT ANSWERS)

1.	C		11.	B
2.	A		12.	C
3.	B		13.	C
4.	B		14.	D
5.	B		15.	A
6.	C		16.	A
7.	A		17.	B
8.	B		18.	C
9.	C		19.	C
10.	D		20.	D

21. C
22. A
23. A
24. B
25. D

PREPARING WRITTEN MATERIALS
EXAMINATION SECTION
TEST 1

DIRECTIONS: Each question contains a sentence. Read each sentence carefully to decide whether it is correct. Then, in the space at the right, mark your answer:
- A. If the sentence is incorrect because of bad grammar or sentence structure;
- B. If the sentence is incorrect because of bad punctuation
- C. If the sentence is incorrect because of bad capitalization
- D. If the sentence is correct.

Each incorrect sentence has only one type of error. Consider a sentence correct if it has no errors, although there may be other correct ways of saying the same thing.

SAMPLE QUESTION i: One of our clerks were promoted yesterday.

The subject of this sentence is *one*, so the verb should be *was promoted* instead of *were promoted*. Since the sentence is incorrect because of bad grammar, the answer to Sample Question I is A.

SAMPLE QUESTION II: Between you and me, I would prefer not going there.

Since this sentence is correct, the answer to Sample Question II is D.

1. The National alliance of Businessmen is trying to persuade private businesses to hire youth in the summertime.   1.____

2. The supervisor who is on vacation, is in charge of processing vouchers.   2.____

3. The activity of the committee at its conferences is always stimulating.   3.____

4. After checking the addresses again, the letters went to the mailroom.   4.____

5. The director, as well as the employees, are interested in sharing the dividends.   5.____

6. The experiments conducted by professor Alford were described at a recent meeting of our organization.   6.____

7. I shall be glad to discuss these matters with whoever represents the Municipal Credit Union.   7.____

8. In my opinion, neither Mr. Price nor Mr. Roth knows how to operate this office appliance.   8.____

9. The supervisor, as well as the other stenographers, were unable to transcribe Miss Johnson's shorthand notes. 9.____

10. Important functions such as, recruiting and training, are performed by our unit. 10.____

11. Realizing that many students are interested in this position, we sent announcements to all the High Schools. 11.____

12. After pointing out certain incorrect conclusions, the report was revised by Mr. Clark and submitted to Mr. Batson. 12.____

13. The employer contributed two hundred dollars; the employees, one hundred dollars. 13.____

14. He realized that the time, when a supervisor could hire and fire, was over. 14.____

15. The complaints received by Commissioner Regan was the cause of the change in policy. 15.____

16. Any report, that is to be sent to the Federal Security Administration, must be approved and signed by Mr. Yound. 16.____

17. Of the two stenographers, Miss Rand is the more accurate. 17.____

18. Since the golf courses are crowded during the summer, more men are needed to maintain the courses in good playing condition. 18.____

19. Although he invited Mr. Frankel and I to attend a meeting of the Civil Service Assembly, we were unable to accept his invitation. 19.____

20. Only the employees who worked overtime last week may leave one hour earlier today. 20.____

21. We need someone who can speak french fluently. 21.____

22. A tall, elderly, man entered the office and asked to see Mr. Brown. 22.____

23. The clerk insisted that he had filed the correspondence in the proper cabinet. 23.____

24. "Will you assist us," he asked? 24.____

25. According to the information contained in the report, a large quantity of paper and envelopes were used by this bureau last year. 25.____

KEY (CORRECT ANSWERS)

1.	C	11.	C
2.	B	12.	A
3.	D	13.	D
4.	A	14.	B
5.	A	15.	A
6.	C	16.	B
7.	D	17.	D
8.	D	18.	C
9.	A	19.	A
10.	B	20.	D

21. C
22. B
23. D
24. B
25. A

TEST 2

DIRECTIONS: Each question consists of a sentence which may be classified appropriately under one of the following four categories:
- A. Incorrect because of faulty grammar or sentence structure.
- B. Incorrect because of faulty punctuation.
- C. Incorrect because of faulty capitalization.
- D. Correct

Examine each sentence carefully. Then, in the space at the right, print the capital letter preceding the option which is the BEST of the four suggested above. All incorrect sentences contain only one type of error. Consider a sentence correct if it contains none of the types of errors mentioned, although there may be other correct ways of expressing the same thought.

1. Mrs. Black the supervisor of the unit, has many important duties. 1._____
2. We spoke to the man whom you saw yesterday. 2._____
3. When a holiday falls on sunday, it is officially celebrated on monday. 3._____
4. Of the two reports submitted, this one is the best. 4._____
5. Each staff member, including the accountants, were invited to the meeting. 5._____
6. Give the package to whomever calls for it. 6._____
7. To plan the work is our responsibility; to carry it out is his. 7._____
8. "May I see the person in charge of this office," asked the visitor? 8._____
9. He knows that it was not us who prepared the report. 9._____
10. These problems were brought to the attention of senator Johnson. 10._____
11. The librarian classifies all books periodicals and documents. 11._____
12. Any employee who uses an adding machine realizes its importance. 12._____
13. Instead of coming to the office, the clerk should of come to the supply room. 13._____
14. He asked, "will your staff assist us?" 14._____
15. Having been posted on the bulletin board, we were certain that the announcements would be read. 15._____
16. He was not informed, that he would have to work overtime. 16._____
17. The wind blew several paper off of his desk. 17._____

18. Charles Dole, who is a member of the committee, was asked to confer with commissioner Wilson. 18.____

19. Miss Bell will issue a copy to whomever asks for one. 19.____

20. Most employees, and he is no exception do not like to work overtime. 20.____

21. This is the man whom you interviewed last week. 21.____

22. Of the two cities visited, White Plains is the cleanest. 22.____

23. Although he was willing to work on other holidays, he refused to work on Labor day. 23.____

24. If an employee wishes to attend the conference, he should fill out the necessary forms. 24.____

25. The division chief reports that an engineer and an inspector is needed for this special survey. 25.____

KEY (CORRECT ANSWERS)

1.	B		11.	B
2.	D		12.	D
3.	C		13.	A
4.	A		14.	C
5.	A		15.	A
6.	A		16.	B
7.	D		17.	A
8.	B		18.	C
9.	A		19.	A
10.	C		20.	B

21. D
22. A
23. C
24. D
25. A

TEST 3

DIRECTIONS: Each question consists of a sentence which may be classified appropriately under one of the following four categories:
- A. Incorrect because of faulty grammar or sentence structure.
- B. Incorrect because of faulty punctuation.
- C. Incorrect because of faulty capitalization.
- D. Correct

Examine each sentence carefully. Then, in the space at the right, print the capital letter preceding the option which is the BEST of the four suggested above. All incorrect sentences contain only one type of error. Consider a sentence correct if it contains none of the types of errors mentioned, although there may be other correct ways of expressing the same thought.

1. We have learned that there was more than twelve people present at the meeting. 1.____

2. Every one of the employees is able to do this kind of work. 2.____

3. Neither the supervisor nor his assistant are in the office today. 3.____

4. The office manager announced that any clerk, who volunteered for the assignment, would be rewarded. 4.____

5. After looking carefully in all the files, the letter was finally found on a desk. 5.____

6. In answer to the clerk's question, the supervisor said, "this assignment must be completed today." 6.____

7. The office manager says that he can permit only you and me to go to the meeting. 7.____

8. The supervisor refused to state who he would assign to the reception unit. 8.____

9. At the last meeting, he said that he would interview us in september. 9.____

10. Mr. Jones, who is one of our most experienced employees has been placed in charge of the main office. 10.____

11. I think that this adding machine is the most useful of the two we have in our office. 11.____

12. Between you and I, our new stenographer is not as competent as our former stenographer. 12.____

13. The new assignment should be given to whoever can do the work rapidly 13.____

14. Mrs. Smith, as well as three other typists, was assigned to the new office. 14.____

2 (#3)

15. The staff assembled for the conference on time but, the main speaker arrived late.   15.____

16. The work was assigned to Miss Green and me.   16.____

17. The staff regulations state that an employee, who is frequently tardy, may receive a negative evaluation.   17.____

18. He is the kind of person who is always willing to undertake difficult assignments.   18.____

19. Mr. Wright's request cannot be granted under no conditions.   19.____

20. George Colt a new employee, was asked to deliver the report to the Domestic Relations Court.   20.____

21. The supervisor entered the room and said, "The work must be completed today."   21.____

22. The employees were given their assignments and, they were asked to begin work immediately.   22.____

23. The letter will be sent to the United States senate this week.   23.____

24. When the supervisor entered the room, he noticed that the book was laying on the desk.   24.____

25. The price of the pens were higher than the price of the pencils.   25.____

KEY (CORRECT ANSWERS)

1.	A		11.	A
2.	D		12.	A
3.	A		13.	D
4.	B		14.	D
5.	A		15.	B
6.	C		16.	D
7.	D		17.	B
8.	A		18.	D
9.	C		19.	A
10.	B		20.	B

21. D
22. B
23. C
24. A
25. A

PREPARING WRITTEN MATERIAL

PARAGRAPH REARRANGEMENT
COMMENTARY

The sentences that follow are in scrambled order. You are to rearrange them in proper order and indicate the letter choice containing the correct answer at the space at the right.

Each group of sentences in this section is actually a paragraph presented in scrambled order. Each sentence in the group has a place in that paragraph; no sentence is to be left out. You are to read each group of sentences and decide upon the best order in which to put the sentences so as to form a well-organized paragraph.

The questions in this section measure the ability to solve a problem when all the facts relevant to its solution are not given.

More specifically, certain positions of responsibility and authority require the employee to discover connection between events sometimes, apparently, unrelated. In order to do this, the employee will find it necessary to correctly infer that unspecified events have probably occurred or are likely to occur. This ability becomes especially important when action must be taken on incomplete information.

Accordingly, these questions require competitors to choose among several suggested alternatives, each of which presents a different sequential arrangement of the events. Competitors must choose the MOST logical of the suggested sequences.

In order to do so, they may be required to draw on general knowledge to infer missing concepts or events that are essential to sequencing the given events. Competitors should be careful to infer only what is essential to the sequence. The plausibility of the wrong alternatives will always require the inclusion of unlikely events or of additional chains of events which are NOT essential to sequencing the given events.

It's very important to remember that you are looking for the best of the four possible choices, and that the best choice of all may not even be one of the answers you're given to choose from.

There is no one right way to solve these problems. Many people have found it helpful to first write out the order of the sentences, as they would have arranged them, on their scrap paper before looking at the possible answers. If their optimum answer is there, this can save them some time. If it isn't, this method can still give insight into solving the problem. Others find it most helpful to just go through each of the possible choices, contrasting each as they go along. You should use whatever method feels comfortable and works for you.

While most of these types of questions are not that difficult, we've added a higher percentage of the difficult type, just to give you more practice. Usually there are only one or two questions on this section that contain such subtle distinctions that you're unable to answer confidently. And you then may find yourself stuck deciding between two possible choices, neither of which you're sure about.

EXAMINATION SECTION
TEST 1

DIRECTIONS: The sentences that follow are in scrambled order. You are to rearrange them in proper order and indicate the letter choice containing the correct answer. *PRINT THE LETTER OF THE CORRECT ANSWER IN THE SPACE AT THE RIGHT.*

1. Below are four statements labeled W, X, Y and Z.
   W. He was a strict and fanatic drillmaster.
   X. The word is always used in a derogatory sense and generally shows resentment and anger on the part of the user.
   Y. It is from the name of this Frenchman that we derive our English word, martinet.
   Z. Jean Martinet was the Inspector-General of Infantry during the reign of King Louis XIV.
   The PROPER order in which these sentences should be placed in a paragraph is:
   A. X, Z, W, Y   B. X, Z, Y, W   C. Z, W, Y, X   D. Z, Y, W, X

   1.____

2. In the following paragraph, the sentences, which are numbered, have been jumbled.
   I. Since then it has undergone changes.
   II. It was incorporated in 1955 under the laws of the State of New York.
   III. Its primary purposes, a cleaner city, has, however, remained the same.
   IV. The Citizens Committee works in cooperation with the Mayor's Inter-departmental Committee for a Clean City.
   The order in which these sentences should be arranged to form a well-organized paragraph is:
   A. II, IV, I, III   B. III, IV, I, II   C. IV, II, I, III   D. IV, III, II, I

   2.____

   3.____

Questions 3-5.

DIRECTIONS: The sentences listed below are part of a meaningful paragraph but they are not given in their proper order. You are to decide what would be the BEST order in which to put the sentences so as to form a well-organized paragraph. Each sentence has a place in the paragraph; there are no extra sentences. You are then to answer Questions 3 through 5 inclusive on the basis of your rearrangements of these scrambled sentences into a properly organized paragraph.

In 1887 some insurance companies organized an Inspection Department to advise their clients on all phases of fire prevention and protection. Probably this has been due to the smaller annual fire losses in Great Britain than in the United States. It tests various fire prevention devices and appliances and determines manufacturing hazards and their safeguards. Fire research began earlier in the United States and is more advanced than in Great Britain. Later they established a laboratory specializing in electrical, mechanical, hydraulic, and chemical fields.

3. When the five sentences are arranged in proper order, the paragraph starts with the sentence which begins
   A. "In 1887..." B. "Probably this..." C. "It tests..."
   D. "Fire research..." E. "Later they..."

3.____

4. In the last sentence listed above, "they" refers to
   A. the insurance companies
   B. the United States and Great Britain
   C. the Inspection Department
   D. clients
   E. technicians

4.____

5. When the above paragraph is properly arranged, it ends with the words
   A. "...and protection."
   B. "...the United States."
   C. "...their safeguards."
   D. "...in Great Britain."
   E. "...chemical fields."

5.____

KEY (CORRECT ANSWERS)

1. C
2. C
3. D
4. A
5. C

TEST 2

DIRECTIONS: In each of the questions numbered I through V, several sentences are given. For each question, choose as your answer the group of number that represents the MOST logical order of these sentences if they were arranged in paragraph form. *PRINT THE LETTER OF THE CORRECT ANSWER IN THE SPACE AT THE RIGHT.*

1. I. It is established when one shows that the landlord has prevented the tenant's enjoyment of his interest in the property leased.
    II. Constructive eviction is the result of a breach of the covenant of quiet enjoyment implied in all leases.
    III. In some parts of the United States, it is not complete until the tenant vacates within a reasonable time.
    IV. Generally, the acts must be of such serious and permanent character as to deny the tenant the enjoyment of his possessing rights.
    V. In this event, upon abandonment of the premises, the tenant's liability for that ceases.
    The CORRECT answer is:
    A. II, I, IV, III, V
    B. V, II, III, I, IV
    C. IV, III, I, II, V
    D. I, III, V, IV, II

1.____

2. I. The powerlessness before private and public authorities that is the typical experience of the slum tenant is reminiscent of the situation of blue-collar workers all through the nineteenth century.
    II. Similarly, in recent years, this chapter of history has been reopened by anti-poverty groups which have attempted to organize slum tenants to enable them to bargain collectively with their landlords about the conditions of their tenancies.
    III. It is familiar history that many of the worker remedied their condition by joining together and presenting their demands collectively.
    IV. Like the workers, tenants are forced by the conditions of modern life into substantial dependence on these who possess great political aid and economic power.
    V. What's more, the very fact of dependence coupled with an absence of education and self-confidence makes them hesitant and unable to stand up for what they need from those in power.
    The CORRECT answer is:
    A. V, IV, I, II, III
    B. II, III, I, V, IV
    C. III, I, V, IV, II
    D. I, IV, V, III, II

2.____

3. I. A railroad, for example, when not acting as a common carrier may contract away responsibility for its own negligence.
    II. As to a landlord, however, no decision has been found relating to the legal effect of a clause shifting the statutory duty of repair to the tenant.
    III. The courts have not passed on the validity of clauses relieving the landlord of this duty and liability.
    IV. They have, however, upheld the validity of exculpatory clauses in other types of contracts.

3.____

109

V. Housing regulations impose a duty upon the landlord to maintain leased premises in safe condition.
VI. As another example, a bailee may limit his liability except for gross negligence, willful acts, or fraud.

The CORRECT answer is:
A. II, I, VI, IV, III, V
B. I, III, IV, V, VI, II
C. III, V, I, IV, II, VI
D. V, III, IV, I, VI, II

4. I. Since there are only samples in the building, retail or consumer sales are generally eschewed by mart occupants, and in some instances, rigid controls are maintained to limit entrance to the mart only to those persons engaged in retailing.
    II. Since World War I, in many larger cities, there has developed a new type of property, called the mart building.
    III. It can, therefore, be used by wholesalers and jobbers for the display of sample merchandise.
    IV. This type of building is most frequently a multi-storied, finished interior property which is a cross between a retail arcade and a loft building.
    V. This limitation enables the mart occupants to ship the orders from another location after the retailer or dealer makes his selection from the samples.

The CORRECT answer is:
A. II, IV, III, I, V
B. IV, III, V, I, II
C. I, III, II, IV, V
D. I, IV, II, III, V

5. I. In general, staff-line friction reduces the distinctive contribution of staff personnel.
    II. The conflicts, however, introduce an uncontrolled element into the managerial system.
    III. On the other hand, the natural resistance of the line to staff innovations probably usefully restrains over-eager efforts to apply untested procedures on a large scale.
    IV. Under such conditions, it is difficult to know when valuable ideas are being sacrificed.
    V. The relatively weak position of staff, requiring accommodation to the line, tends to restrict their ability to engage in free, experimental innovation.

The CORRECT answer is:
A. IV, II, III, I, V
B. I, V, III, II, IV
C. V, III, I, II, IV
D. II, I, IV, V, III

KEY (CORRECT ANSWERS)

1. A
2. D
3. D
4. A
5. B

TEST 3

DIRECTIONS: Questions 1 through 4 consist of six sentences which can be arranged in a logical sequence. For each question, select the choice which places the numbered sentences in the MOST logical sequent. *PRINT THE LETTER OF THE CORRECT ANSWER IN THE SPACE AT THE RIGHT.*

1.
   I. The burden of proof as to each issue is determined before trial and remains upon the same party throughout the trial.
   II. The jury is at liberty to believe one witness' testimony as against a number of contradictory witnesses.
   III. In a civil case, the party bearing the burden of proof is required to prove his contention by a fair preponderance of the evidence.
   IV. However, it must be noted that a fair preponderance of evidence does not necessarily mean a greater number of witnesses.
   V. The burden of proof is the burden which rests upon one of the parties to an action to persuade the trier of the facts, generally the jury, that a proposition he asserts is true.
   VI. If the evidence is equally balanced, or if it leaves the jury in such doubt as to be unable to decide the controversy either way, judgment must be given against the party upon whom the burden of proof rests.
   The CORRECT answer is:
   A. III, II, V, IV, I, VI   B. I, II, VI, V, III, IV
   C. III, IV, V, I, II, VI   D. V, I, III, VI, IV, II

   1.____

2.
   I. If a parent is without assets and is unemployed, he cannot be convicted of the crime of non-support of a child.
   II. The term "sufficient ability" has been held to mean sufficient financial ability.
   III. It does not matter if his unemployment is by choice or unavoidable circumstances.
   IV. If he fails to take any steps at all, he may be liable to prosecution for endangering the welfare of a child.
   V. Under the penal law, a parent is responsible for the support of his minor child only if the parent is "of sufficient ability."
   VI. An indigent parent may meet his obligation by borrowing money or by seeking aid under the provisions of the Social Welfare Law.
   The CORRECT answer is:
   A. VI, I, V, III, II, IV   B. I, III, V, II, IV, VI
   C. V, II, I, III, VI, IV   D. I, VI, IV, V, II, III

   2.____

3.
   I. Consider, for example, the case of a rabble rouser who urges a group of twenty people to go out and break the windows of a nearby factory.
   II. Therefore, the law fills the indicated gap with the crime of inciting to riot.
   III. A person is considered guilty of inciting to riot when he urges ten or more persons to engage in tumultuous and violent conduct of a kind likely to create public alarm.
   IV. However, if he has not obtained the cooperation of at least four people, he cannot be charged with unlawful assembly.

   3.____

111

V. The charge of inciting to riot was added to the law to cover types of conduct which cannot be classified as either the crime of "riot" or the crime of "unlawful assembly."
VI. If he acquires the acquiescence of at least four of them, he is guilty of unlawful assembly even if the project does not materialize.

The CORRECT answer is:
A. III, V, I, VI, IV, II
B. V, I, IV, VI, II, III
C. III, IV, I, V, II, VI
D. V, I, IV, VI, III, II

4. I. If, however, the rebuttal evidence presents an issue of credibility, it is for the jury to determine whether the presumption has, in fact, been destroyed.
II. Once sufficient evidence to the contrary is introduced, the presumption disappears from the trial.
III. The effect of a presumption is to place the burden upon the adversary to come forward with evidence to rebut the presumption.
IV. When a presumption is overcome and ceases to exist in the case, the fact or facts which gave rise to the presumption still remain.
V. Whether a presumption has been overcome is ordinarily a question for the court.
VI. Such information may furnish a basis for a logical inference.

The CORRECT answer is:
A. IV, VI, II, V, I, III
B. III, II, V, I, IV, VI
C. V, III, VI, IV, II, I
D. V, IV, I, II, VI, III

KEY (CORRECT ANSWERS)

1. D
2. C
3. A
4. B

PHILOSOPHY, PRINCIPLES, PRACTICES, AND TECHNICS OF SUPERVISION, ADMINISTRATION, MANAGEMENT, AND ORGANIZATION

TABLE OF CONTENTS

	Page
MEANING OF SUPERVISION	1
THE OLD AND THE NEW SUPERVISION	1
THE EIGHT (8) BASIC PRINCIPLES OF THE NEW SUPERVISION	1
I. Principle of Responsibility	1
II. Principle of Authority	2
III. Principle of Self-Growth	2
IV. Principle of Individual Worth	2
V. Principle of Creative Leadership	2
VI. Principle of Success and Failure	2
VII. Principle of Science	3
VIII. Principle of Cooperation	3
WHAT IS ADMINISTRATION?	3
I. Practices Commonly Classed as "Supervisory"	3
II. Practices Commonly Classed as "Administrative"	3
III. Practices Commonly Classed as Both "Supervisory" and "Administrative"	4
RESPONSIBILITIES OF THE SUPERVISOR	4
COMPETENCIES OF THE SUPERVISOR	4
THE PROFESSIONAL SUPERVISOR-EMPLOYEE RELATIONSHIP	4
MINI-TEXT IN SUPERVISION, ADMINISTRATION, MANAGEMENT, AND ORGANIZATION	5
I. Brief Highlights	5
A. Levels of Management	6
B. What the Supervisor Must Learn	6
C. A Definition of Supervision	6
D. Elements of the Team Concept	6
E. Principles of Organization	6
F. The Four Important Parts of Every Job	7
G. Principles of Delegation	7
H. Principles of Effective Communications	7
I. Principles of Work Improvement	7
J. Areas of Job Improvement	7
K. Seven Key Points in Making Improvements	8

L.	Corrective Techniques for Job Improvement	8
M.	A Planning Checklist	8
N.	Five Characteristics of Good Directions	9
O.	Types of Directions	9
P.	Controls	9
Q.	Orienting the New Employee	9
R.	Checklist for Orienting New Employees	9
S.	Principles of Learning	10
T.	Causes of Poor Performance	10
U.	Four Major Steps in On-the-Job Instructions	10
V.	Employees Want Five Things	10
W.	Some Don'ts in Regard to Praise	11
X.	How to Gain Your Workers' Confidence	11
Y.	Sources of Employee Problems	11
Z.	The Supervisor's Key to Discipline	11
AA.	Five Important Processes of Management	12
BB.	When the Supervisor Fails to Plan	12
CC.	Fourteen General Principles of Management	12
DD.	Change	12

II. Brief Topical Summaries — 13
- A. Who/What is the Supervisor? — 13
- B. The Sociology of Work — 13
- C. Principles and Practices of Supervision — 14
- D. Dynamic Leadership — 14
- E. Processes for Solving Problems — 15
- F. Training for Results — 15
- G. Health, Safety, and Accident Prevention — 16
- H. Equal Employment Opportunity — 16
- I. Improving Communications — 16
- J. Self-Development — 17
- K. Teaching and Training — 17
  1. The Teaching Process — 17
     a. Preparation — 17
     b. Presentation — 18
     c. Summary — 18
     d. Application — 18
     e. Evaluation — 18
  2. Teaching Methods — 18
     a. Lecture — 18
     b. Discussion — 18
     c. Demonstration — 19
     d. Performance — 19
     e. Which Method to Use — 19

PHILOSOPHY, PRINCIPLES, PRACTICES, AND TECHNICS OF SUPERVISION, ADMINISTRATION, MANAGEMENT, AND ORGANIZATION

MEANING OF SUPERVISION

The extension of the democratic philosophy has been accompanied by an extension in the scope of supervision. Modern leaders and supervisors no longer think of supervision in the narrow sense of being confined chiefly to visiting employees, supplying materials, or rating the staff. They regard supervision as being intimately related to all the concerned agencies of society, they speak of the supervisor's function in terms of "growth," rather than the "improvement" of employees.

This modern concept of supervision may be defined as follows: Supervision is leadership and the development of leadership within groups which are cooperatively engaged in inspection, research, training, guidance, and evaluation.

THE OLD AND THE NEW SUPERVISION

TRADITIONAL
1. Inspection
2. Focused on the employee
3. Visitation
4. Random and haphazard
5. Imposed and authoritarian
6. One person usually

MODERN
1. Study and analysis
2. Focused on aims, materials, methods, supervisors, employees, environment
3. Demonstrations, intervisitation, workshops, directed reading, bulletins, etc.
4. Definitely organized and planned (scientific)
5. Cooperative and democratic
6. Many persons involved (creative)

THE EIGHT (8) BASIC PRINCIPLES OF THE NEW SUPERVISION

I. Principle of Responsibility
   Authority to act and responsibility for acting must be joined.
   A. If you give responsibility, give authority.
   B. Define employee duties clearly.
   C. Protect employees from criticism by others.
   D. Recognize the rights as well as obligations of employees.
   E. Achieve the aims of a democratic society insofar as it is possible within the area of your work.
   F. Establish a situation favorable to training and learning.
   G. Accept ultimate responsibility for everything done in your section, unit, office, division, department.
   H. Good administration and good supervision are inseparable.

II. Principle of Authority
The success of the supervisor is measured by the extent to which the power of authority is not used.
   A. Exercise simplicity and informality in supervision
   B. Use the simplest machinery of supervision
   C. If it is good for the organization as a whole, it is probably justified.
   D. Seldom be arbitrary or authoritative.
   E. Do not base your work on the power of position or of personality.
   F. Permit and encourage the free expression of opinions.

III. Principle of Self-Growth
The success of the supervisor is measured by the extent to which, and the speed with which, he is no longer needed.
   A. Base criticism on principles, not on specifics.
   B. Point out higher activities to employees.
   C. Train for self-thinking by employees to meet new situations.
   D. Stimulate initiative, self-reliance, and individual responsibility
   E. Concentrate on stimulating the growth of employees rather than on removing defects.

IV. Principle of Individual Worth
Respect for the individual is a paramount consideration in supervision.
   A. Be human and sympathetic in dealing with employees.
   B. Don't nag about things to be done.
   C. Recognize the individual differences among employees and seek opportunities to permit best expression of each personality.

V. Principle of Creative Leadership
The best supervision is that which is not apparent to the employee.
   A. Stimulate, don't drive employees to creative action.
   B. Emphasize doing good things.
   C. Encourage employees to do what they do best.
   D. Do not be too greatly concerned with details of subject or method.
   E. Do not be concerned exclusively with immediate problems and activities.
   F. Reveal higher activities and make them both desired and maximally possible.
   G. Determine procedures in the light of each situation but see that these are derived from a sound basic philosophy.
   H. Aid, inspire, and lead so as to liberate the creative spirit latent in all good employees.

VI. Principle of Success and Failure
There are no unsuccessful employees, only unsuccessful supervisors who have failed to give proper leadership.
   A. Adapt suggestions to the capacities, attitudes, and prejudices of employees.
   B. Be gradual, be progressive, be persistent.
   C. Help the employee find the general principle; have the employee apply his own problem to the general principle.
   D. Give adequate appreciation for good work and honest effort.
   E. Anticipate employee difficulties and help to prevent them.
   F. Encourage employees to do the desirable things they will do anyway.
   G. Judge your supervision by the results it secures.

VII. Principle of Science
Successful supervision is scientific, objective, and experimental. It is based on facts, not on prejudices.
   A.   Be cumulative in results.
   B.   Never divorce your suggestions from the goals of training.
   C.   Don't be impatient of results.
   D.   Keep all matters on a professional, not a personal, level.
   E.   Do not be concerned exclusively with immediate problems and activities.
   F.   Use objective means of determining achievement and rating where possible.

VIII. Principle of Cooperation
Supervision is a cooperative enterprise between supervisor and employee.
   A.   Begin with conditions as they are.
   B.   Ask opinions of all involved when formulating policies.
   C.   Organization is as good as its weakest link.
   D.   Let employees help to determine policies and department programs.
   E.   Be approachable and accessible—physically and mentally.
   F.   Develop pleasant social relationships.

WHAT IS ADMINISTRATION

Administration is concerned with providing the environment, the material facilities, and the operational procedures that will promote the maximum growth and development of supervisors and employees. (Organization is an aspect and a concomitant of administration.)

There is no sharp line of demarcation between supervision and administration; these functions are intimately interrelated and, often, overlapping. They are complementary activities.

I.   Practices Commonly Classed as "Supervisory"
   A.   Conducting employees' conferences
   B.   Visiting sections, units, offices, divisions, departments
   C.   Arranging for demonstrations
   D.   Examining plans
   E.   Suggesting professional reading
   F.   Interpreting bulletins
   G.   Recommending in-service training courses
   H.   Encouraging experimentation
   I.   Appraising employee morale
   J.   Providing for intervisitation

II.   Practices Commonly Classified as "Administrative"
   A.   Management of the office
   B.   Arrangement of schedules for extra duties
   C.   Assignment of rooms or areas
   D.   Distribution of supplies
   E.   Keeping records and reports
   F.   Care of audio-visual materials
   G.   Keeping inventory records
   H.   Checking record cards and books

I. Programming special activities
J. Checking on the attendance and punctuality of employees

III. Practices Commonly Classified as Both "Supervisory" and "Administrative"
   A. Program construction
   B. Testing or evaluating outcomes
   C. Personnel accounting
   D. Ordering instructional materials

RESPONSIBILITIES OF THE SUPERVISOR

A person employed in a supervisory capacity must constantly be able to improve his own efficiency and ability. He represent the employer to the employees and only continuous self-examination can make him a capable supervisor.

Leadership and training are the supervisor's responsibility. An efficient working unit is one in which the employees work with the supervisor. It is his job to bring out the best in his employees. He must always be relaxed, courteous, and calm in his association with his employees. Their feelings are important, and a harsh attitude does not develop the most efficient employees.

COMPETENCES OF THE SUPERVISOR

I. Complete knowledge of the duties and responsibilities of his position.
II. To be able to organize a job, plan ahead, and carry through.
III. To have self-confidence and initiative.
IV. To be able to handle the unexpected situation and make quick decisions.
V. To be able to properly train subordinates in the positions they are best suited for.
VI. To be able to keep good human relations among his subordinates.
VII. To be able to keep good human relations between his subordinates and himself and to earn their respect and trust.

THE PROFESSIONAL SUPERVISOR-EMPLOYEE RELATIONSHIP

There are two kinds of efficiency: one kind is only apparent and is produced in organizations through the exercise of mere discipline; this is but a simulation of the second, or true, efficiency which springs from spontaneous cooperation. If you are a manager, no matter how great or small your responsibility, it is your job, in the final analysis, to create and develop this involuntary cooperation among the people whom you supervise. For, no matter how powerful a combination of money, machines, and materials a company may have, this is a dead and sterile thing without a team of willing, thinking, and articulate people to guide it.

The following 21 points are presented as indicative of the exemplary basic relationship that should exist between supervisor and employee:

1. Each person wants to be liked and respected by his fellow employee and wants to be treated with consideration and respect by his superior.
2. The most competent employee will make an error. However, in a unit where good relations exist between the supervisor and his employees, tenseness and fear do not exist. Thus, errors are not hidden or covered up, and the efficiency of a unit is not impaired.

3. Subordinates resent rules, regulations, or orders that are unreasonable or unexplained.
4. Subordinates are quick to resent unfairness, harshness, injustices, and favoritism.
5. An employee will accept responsibility if he knows that he will be complimented for a job well done, and not too harshly chastised for failure; that his supervisor will check the cause of the failure, and, if it was the supervisor's fault, he will assume the blame therefore. If it was the employee's fault, his supervisor will explain the correct method or means of handling the responsibility.
6. An employee wants to receive credit for a suggestion he has made, that is used. If a suggestion cannot be used, the employee is entitled to an explanation. The supervisor should not say "no" and close the subject.
7. Fear and worry slow up a worker's ability. Poor working environment can impair his physical and mental health. A good supervisor avoids forceful methods, threats, and arguments to get a job done.
8. A forceful supervisor is able to train his employees individually and as a team, and is able to motivate them in the proper channels.
9. A mature supervisor is able to properly evaluate his subordinates and to keep them happy and satisfied.
10. A sensitive supervisor will never patronize his subordinates.
11. A worthy supervisor will respect his employees' confidences.
12. Definite and clear-cut responsibilities should be assigned to each executive.
13. Responsibility should always be coupled with corresponding authority.
14. No change should be made in the scope or responsibilities of a position without a definite understanding to that effect on the part of all persons concerned.
15. No executive or employee, occupying a single position in the organization, should be subject to definite orders from more than one source.
16. Orders should never be given to subordinates over the head of a responsible executive. Rather than do this, the officer in question should be supplanted.
17. Criticisms of subordinates should, whoever possible, be made privately, and in no case should a subordinate be criticized in the presence of executives or employees of equal or lower rank.
18. No dispute or difference between executives or employees as to authority or responsibilities should be considered too trivial for prompt and careful adjudication.
19. Promotions, wage changes, and disciplinary action should always be approved by the executive immediately superior to the one directly responsible.
20. No executive or employee should ever be required, or expected, to be at the same time an assistant to, and critic of, another.
21. Any executive whose work is subject to regular inspection should, wherever practicable, be given the assistance and facilities necessary to enable him to maintain an independent check of the quality of his work.

MINI-TEXT IN SUPERVISION, ADMINISTRATION, MANAGEMENT, AND ORGANIZATION

I. Brief Highlights

Listed concisely and sequentially are major headings and important data in the field for quick recall and review.

A. Levels of Management
Any organization of some size has several levels of management. In terms of a ladder, the levels are:

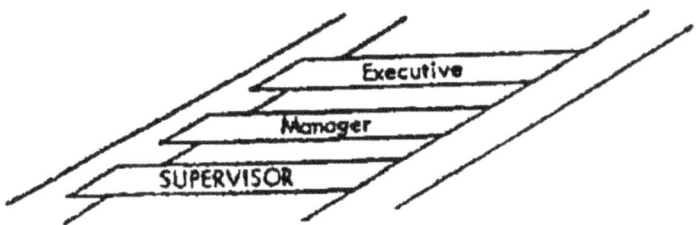

The first level is very important because it is the beginning point of management leadership.

B. What the Supervisor Must Learn
A supervisor must learn to:
1. Deal with people and their differences
2. Get the job done through people
3. Recognize the problems when they exist
4. Overcome obstacles to good performance
5. Evaluate the performance of people
6. Check his own performance in terms of accomplishment

C. A Definition of Supervisor
The term supervisor means any individual having authority, in the interests of the employer, to hire, transfer, suspend, lay-off, recall, promote, discharge, assign, reward, or discipline other employees or responsibility to direct them, or to adjust their grievances, or effectively to recommend such action, if, in connection with the foregoing, exercise of such authority is not of a merely routine or clerical nature but requires the use of independent judgment.

D. Elements of the Team Concept
What is involved in teamwork? The component parts are:
1. Members
2. A leader
3. Goals
4. Plans
5. Cooperation
6. Spirit

E. Principles of Organization
1. A team member must know what his job is.
2. Be sure that the nature and scope of a job are understood.
3. Authority and responsibility should be carefully spelled out.
4. A supervisor should be permitted to make the maximum number of decisions affecting his employees.
5. Employees should report to only one supervisor.
6. A supervisor should direct only as many employees as he can handle effectively.
7. An organization plan should be flexible.

8. Inspection and performance of work should be separate.
9. Organizational problems should receive immediate attention.
10. Assign work in line with ability and experience.

F. The Four Important Parts of Every Job
1. Inherent in every job is the *accountability* for results.
2. A second set of factors in every job is *responsibilities*.
3. Along with duties and responsibilities one must have the *authority* to act within certain limits without obtaining permission to proceed.
4. No job exists in a vacuum. The supervisor is surrounded by key *relationships*.

G. Principles of Delegation
Where work is delegated for the first time, the supervisor should think in terms of these questions:
1. Who is best qualified to do this?
2. Can an employee improve his abilities by doing this?
3. How long should an employee spend on this?
4. Are there any special problems for which he will need guidance?
5. How broad a delegation can I make?

H. Principles of Effective Communications
1. Determine the media.
2. To whom directed?
3. Identification and source authority.
4. Is communication understood?

I. Principles of Work Improvement
1. Most people usually do only the work which is assigned to them.
2. Workers are likely to fit assigned work into the time available to perform it.
3. A good workload usually stimulates output.
4. People usually do their best work when they know that results will be reviewed or inspected.
5. Employees usually feel that someone else is responsible for conditions of work, workplace layout, job methods, type of tools/equipment, and other such factors.
6. Employees are usually defensive about their job security.
7. Employees have natural resistance to change.
8. Employees can support or destroy a supervisor.
9. A supervisor usually earns the respect of his people through his personal example of diligence and efficiency.

J. Areas of Job Improvement
The areas of job improvement are quite numerous, but the most common ones which a supervisor can identify and utilize are:
1. Departmental layout
2. Flow of work
3. Workplace layout
4. Utilization of manpower
5. Work methods
6. Materials handling

7. Utilization
8. Motion economy

K. Seven Key Points in Making Improvements
1. Select the job to be improved
2. Study how it is being done now
3. Question the present method
4. Determine actions to be taken
5. Chart proposed method
6. Get approval and apply
7. Solicit worker participation

I. Corrective Techniques of Job Improvement
Specific Problems
1. Size of workload
2. Inability to meet schedules
3. Strain and fatigue
4. Improper use of men and skills
5. Waste, poor quality, unsafe conditions
6. Bottleneck conditions that hinder output
7. Poor utilization of equipment and machine
8. Efficiency and productivity of labor

General Improvement
1. Departmental layout
2. Flow of work
3. Work plan layout
4. Utilization of manpower
5. Work methods
6. Materials handling
7. Utilization of equipment
8. Motion economy

Corrective Techniques
1. Study with scale model
2. Flow chart study
3. Motion analysis
4. Comparison of units produced to standard allowance
5. Methods analysis
6. Flow chart and equipment study
7. Down time vs. running time
8. Motion analysis

M. A Planning Checklist
1. Objectives
2. Controls
3. Delegations
4. Communications
5. Resources
6. Manpower

7. Equipment
8. Supplies and materials
9. Utilization of time
10. Safety
11. Money
12. Work
13. Timing of improvements

N. Five Characteristics of Good Directions
In order to get results, directions must be:
1. Possible of accomplishment
2. Agreeable with worker interests
3. Related to mission
4. Planned and complete
5. Unmistakably clear

O. Types of Directions
1. Demands or direct orders
2. Requests
3. Suggestion or implication
4. volunteering

P. Controls
A typical listing of the overall areas in which the supervisor should establish controls might be:
1. Manpower
2. Materials
3. Quality of work
4. Quantity of work
5. Time
6. Space
7. Money
8. Methods

Q. Orienting the New Employee
1. Prepare for him
2. Welcome the new employee
3. Orientation for the job
4. Follow-up

R. Checklist for Orienting New Employees   Yes   No
1. Do you appreciate the feelings of new employees when they first report for work?   ___   ___
2. Are you aware of the fact that the new employee must make a big adjustment to his job?   ___   ___
3. Have you given him good reasons for liking the job and the organization?   ___   ___
4. Have you prepared for his first day on the job?   ___   ___
5. Did you welcome him cordially and make him feel needed?   ___   ___

		Yes	No

6. Did you establish rapport with him so that he feels free to talk and discuss matters with you? ___ ___
7. Did you explain his job to him and his relationship to you? ___ ___
8. Does he know that his work will be evaluated periodically on a basis that is fair and objective? ___ ___
9. Did you introduce him to his fellow workers in such a way that they are likely to accept him? ___ ___
10. Does he know what employee benefits he will receive? ___ ___
11. Does he understand the importance of being on the job and what to do if he must leave his duty station? ___ ___
12. Has he been impressed with the importance of accident prevention and safe practice? ___ ___
13. Does he generally know his way around the department? ___ ___
14. Is he under the guidance of a sponsor who will teach the right way of doing things? ___ ___
15. Do you plan to follow-up so that he will continue to adjust successfully to his job? ___ ___

S. Principles of Learning
1. Motivation
2. Demonstration or explanation
3. Practice

T. Causes of Poor Performance
1. Improper training for job
2. Wrong tools
3. Inadequate directions
4. Lack of supervisory follow-up
5. Poor communications
6. Lack of standards of performance
7. Wrong work habits
8. Low morale
9. Other

U. Four Major Steps in On-The-Job Instruction
1. Prepare the worker
2. Present the operation
3. Tryout performance
4. Follow-up

V. Employees Want Five Things
1. Security
2. Opportunity
3. Recognition
4. Inclusion
5. Expression

W. Some Don'ts in Regard to Praise
1. Don't praise a person for something he hasn't done.
2. Don't praise a person unless you can be sincere.
3. Don't be sparing in praise just because your superior withholds it from you.
4. Don't let too much time elapse between good performance and recognition of it

X. How to Gain Your Workers' Confidence
Methods of developing confidence include such things as:
1. Knowing the interests, habits, hobbies of employees
2. Admitting your own inadequacies
3. Sharing and telling of confidence in others
4. Supporting people when they are in trouble
5. Delegating matters that can be well handled
6. Being frank and straightforward about problems and working conditions
7. Encouraging others to bring their problems to you
8. Taking action on problems which impede worker progress

Y. Sources of Employee Problems
On-the-job causes might be such things as:
1. A feeling that favoritism is exercised in assignments
2. Assignment of overtime
3. An undue amount of supervision
4. Changing methods or systems
5. Stealing of ideas or trade secrets
6. Lack of interest in job
7. Threat of reduction in force
8. Ignorance or lack of communications
9. Poor equipment
10. Lack of knowing how supervisor feels toward employee
11. Shift assignments

Off-the-job problems might have to do with:
1. Health
2. Finances
3. Housing
4. Family

Z. The Supervisor's Key to Discipline
There are several key points about discipline which the supervisor should keep in mind:
1. Job discipline is one of the disciplines of life and is directed by the supervisor.
2. It is more important to correct an employee fault than to fix blame for it.
3. Employee performance is affected by problems both on the job and off.
4. Sudden or abrupt changes in behavior can be indications of important employee problems.
5. Problems should be dealt with as soon as possible after they are identified.
6. The attitude of the supervisor may have more to do with solving problems than the techniques of problem solving.
7. Correction of employee behavior should be resorted to only after the supervisor is sure that training or counseling will not be helpful.

8. Be sure to document your disciplinary actions.
9. Make sure that you are disciplining on the basis of facts rather than personal feelings.
10. Take each disciplinary step in order, being careful not to make snap judgments, or decisions based on impatience.

AA. Five Important Processes of Management
1. Planning
2. Organizing
3. Scheduling
4. Controlling
5. Motivating

BB. When the Supervisor Fails to Plan
1. Supervisor creates impression of not knowing his job
2. May lead to excessive overtime
3. Job runs itself—supervisor lacks control
4. Deadlines and appointments missed
5. Parts of the work go undone
6. Work interrupted by emergencies
7. Sets a bad example
8. Uneven workload creates peaks and valleys
9. Too much time on minor details at expense of more important tasks

CC. Fourteen General Principles of Management
1. Division of work
2. Authority and responsibility
3. Discipline
4. Unity of command
5. Unity of direction
6. Subordination of individual interest to general interest
7. Remuneration of personnel
8. Centralization
9. Scalar chain
10. Order
11. Equity
12. Stability of tenure of personnel
13. Initiative
14. Esprit de corps

DD. Change

Bringing about change is perhaps attempted more often, and yet less well understood, than anything else the supervisor does. How do people generally react to change? (People tend to resist change that is imposed upon them by other individuals or circumstances.

Change is characteristic of every situation. It is a part of every real endeavor where the efforts of people are concerned.

1. Why do people resist change?
   People may resist change because of:
   a. Fear of the unknown
   b. Implied criticism
   c. Unpleasant experiences in the past
   d. Fear of loss of status
   e. Threat to the ego
   f. Fear of loss of economic stability

2. How can we best overcome the resistance to change?
   In initiating change, take these steps:
   a. Get ready to sell
   b. Identify sources of help
   c. Anticipate objections
   d. Sell benefits
   e. Listen in depth
   f. Follow up

II. Brief Topical Summaries

   A. Who/What is the Supervisor?
      1. The supervisor is often called the "highest level employee and the lowest level manager."
      2. A supervisor is a member of both management and the work group. He acts as a bridge between the two.
      3. Most problems in supervision are in the area of human relations, or people problems.
      4. Employees expect: Respect, opportunity to learn and to advance, and a sense of belonging, and so forth.
      5. Supervisors are responsible for directing people and organizing work. Planning is of paramount importance.
      6. A position description is a set of duties and responsibilities inherent to a given position.
      7. It is important to keep the position description up-to-date and to provide each employee with his own copy.

   B. The Sociology of Work
      1. People are alike in many ways; however, each individual is unique.
      2. The supervisor is challenged in getting to know employee differences. Acquiring skills in evaluating individuals is an asset.
      3. Maintaining meaningful working relationships in the organization is of great importance.
      4. The supervisor has an obligation to help individuals to develop to their fullest potential.
      5. Job rotation on a planned basis helps to build versatility and to maintain interest and enthusiasm in work groups.
      6. Cross training (job rotation) provides backup skills.

7. The supervisor can help reduce tension by maintaining a sense of humor, providing guidance to employees, and by making reasonable and timely decisions. Employees respond favorably to working under reasonably predictable circumstances.
8. Change is characteristic of all managerial behavior. The supervisor must adjust to changes in procedures, new methods, technological changes, and to a number of new and sometimes challenging situations.
9. To overcome the natural tendency for people to resist change, the supervisor should become more skillful in initiating change.

C. Principles and Practices of Supervision
1. Employees should be required to answer to only one superior.
2. A supervisor can effectively direct only a limited number of employees, depending upon the complexity, variety, and proximity of the jobs involved.
3. The organizational chart presents the organization in graphic form. It reflects lines of authority and responsibility as well as interrelationships of units within the organization.
4. Distribution of work can be improved through an analysis using the "Work Distribution Chart."
5. The "Work Distribution Chart" reflects the division of work within a unit in understandable form.
6. When related tasks are given to an employee, he has a better chance of increasing his skills through training.
7. The individual who is given the responsibility for tasks must also be given the appropriate authority to insure adequate results.
8. The supervisor should delegate repetitive, routine work. Preparation of recurring reports, maintaining leave and attendance records are some examples.
9. Good discipline is essential to good task performance. Discipline is reflected in the actions of employees on the job in the absence of supervision.
10. Disciplinary action may have to be taken when the positive aspects of discipline have failed. Reprimand, warning, and suspension are examples of disciplinary action.
11. If a situation calls for a reprimand, be sure it is deserved and remember it is to be done in private.

D. Dynamic Leadership
1. A style is a personal method or manner of exerting influence.
2. Authoritarian leaders often see themselves as the source of power and authority.
3. The democratic leader often perceives the group as the source of authority and power.
4. Supervisors tend to do better when using the pattern of leadership that is most natural for them.
5. Social scientists suggest that the effective supervisor use the leadership style that best fits the problem or circumstances involved.
6. All four styles—telling, selling, consulting, joining—have their place. Using one does not preclude using the other at another time.

7. The theory X point of view assumes that the average person dislikes work, will avoid it whenever possible, and must be coerced to achieve organizational objectives.
8. The theory Y point of view assumes that the average person considers work to be a natural as play, and, when the individual is committed, he requires little supervision or direction to accomplish desired objectives.
9. The leader's basic assumptions concerning human behavior and human nature affect his actions, decisions, and other managerial practices.
10. Dissatisfaction among employees is often present, but difficult to isolate. The supervisor should seek to weaken dissatisfaction by keeping promises, being sincere and considerate, keeping employees informed, and so forth.
11. Constructive suggestions should be encouraged during the natural progress of the work.

E. Processes for Solving Problems
1. People find their daily tasks more meaningful and satisfying when they can improve them.
2. The causes of problems, or the key factors, are often hidden in the background. Ability to solve problems often involves the ability to isolate them from their backgrounds. There is some substance to the cliché that some persons "can't see the forest for the trees."
3. New procedures are often developed from old ones. Problems should be broken down into manageable parts. New ideas can be adapted from old one.
4. People think differently in problem-solving situations. Using a logical, patterned approach is often useful. One approach found to be useful includes these steps:
   a. Define the problem
   b. Establish objectives
   c. Get the facts
   d. Weigh and decide
   e. Take action
   f. Evaluate action

F. Training for Results
1. Participants respond best when they feel training is important to them.
2. The supervisor has responsibility for the training and development of those who report to him.
3. When training is delegated to others, great care must be exercised to insure the trainer has knowledge, aptitude, and interest for his work as a trainer.
4. Training (learning) of some type goes on continually. The most successful supervisor makes certain the learning contributes in a productive manner to operational goals.
5. New employees are particularly susceptible to training. Older employees facing new job situations require specific training, as well as having need for development and growth opportunities.
6. Training needs require continuous monitoring.
7. The training officer of an agency is a professional with a responsibility to assist supervisors in solving training problems.

8. Many of the self-development steps important to the supervisor's own growth are equally important to the development of peers and subordinates. Knowledge of these is important when the supervisor consults with others on development and growth opportunities.

G. Health, Safety, and Accident Prevention
1. Management-minded supervisors take appropriate measures to assist employees in maintaining health and in assuring safe practices in the work environment.
2. Effective safety training and practices help to avoid injury and accidents.
3. Safety should be a management goal. All infractions of safety which are observed should be corrected without exception.
4. Employees' safety attitude, training and instruction, provision of safe tools and equipment, supervision, and leadership are considered highly important factors which contribute to safety and which can be influenced directly by supervisors.
5. When accidents do occur, they should be investigated promptly for very important reasons, including the fact that information which is gained can be used to prevent accidents in the future.

H. Equal Employment Opportunity
1. The supervisor should endeavor to treat all employees fairly, without regard to religion, race, sex, or national origin.
2. Groups tend to reflect the attitude of the leader. Prejudice can be detected even in very subtle form. Supervisors must strive to create a feeling of mutual respect and confidence in every employee.
3. Complete utilization of all human resources is a national goal. Equitable consideration should be accorded women in the work force, minority-group members, the physically and mentally handicapped, and the older employee. The important question is: "Who can do the job?"
4. Training opportunities, recognition for performance, overtime assignments, promotional opportunities, and all other personnel actions are to be handled on an equitable basis.

I. Improving Communications
1. Communications is achieving understanding between the sender and the receiver of a message. It also means sharing information—the creation of understanding.
2. Communication is basic to all human activity. Words are means of conveying meanings; however, real meanings are in people.
3. There are very practical differences in the effectiveness of one-way, impersonal, and two-way communications. Words spoken face-to-face are better understood. Telephone conversations are effective, but lack the rapport of person-to-person exchanges. The whole person communicates.
4. Cooperation and communication in an organization go hand in hand. When there is a mutual respect between people, spelling out rules and procedures for communicating is unnecessary.
5. There are several barriers to effective communications. These include failure to listen with respect and understanding, lack of skill in feedback, and misinterpreting the meanings of words used by the speaker. It is also common

practice to listen to what we want to hear, and tune out things we do not want to hear.
6. Communication is management's chief problem. The supervisor should accept the challenge to communicate more effectively and to improve interagency and intra-agency communications.
7. The supervisor may often plan for and conduct meetings. The planning phase is critical and may determine the success or the failure of a meeting.
8. Speaking before groups usually requires extra effort. Stage fright may never disappear completely, but it can be controlled.

J. Self-Development
1. Every employee is responsible for his own self-development.
2. Toastmaster and toastmistress clubs offer opportunities to improve skills in oral communications.
3. Planning for one's own self-development is of vital importance. Supervisors know their own strengths and limitations better than anyone else.
4. Many opportunities are open to aid the supervisor in his developmental efforts, including job assignments; training opportunities, both governmental and non-governmental—to include universities and professional conferences and seminars.
5. Programmed instruction offers a means of studying at one's own rate.
6. Where difficulties may arise from a supervisor's being away from his work for training, he may participate in televised home study or correspondence courses to meet his self-development needs.

K. Teaching and Training
1. The Teaching Process
Teaching is encouraging and guiding the learning activities of students toward established goals. In most cases this process consists of five steps: preparation, presentation, summarization, evaluation, and application.

   a. Preparation
   Preparation is two-fold in nature; that of the supervisor and the employee. Preparation by the supervisor is absolutely essential to success. He must know what, when, where, how, and whom he will teach. Some of the factors that should be considered are:
   1) The objectives
   2) The materials needed
   3) The methods to be used
   4) Employee participation
   5) Employee interest
   6) Training aids
   7) Evaluation
   8) Summarization

   Employee preparation consists in preparing the employee to receive the material. Probably the most important single factor in the preparation of the employee is arousing and maintaining his interest. He must know the objectives of the training, why he is there, how the material can be used, and its importance to him.

b. Presentation
In presentation, have a carefully designed plan and follow it. The plan should be accurate and complete, yet flexible enough to meet situations as they arise. The method of presentation will be determined by the particular situation and objectives.

c. Summary
A summary should be made at the end of every training unit and program. In addition, there may be internal summaries depending on the nature of the material being taught. The important thing is that the trainee must always be able to understand how each part of the new material relates to the whole.

d. Application
The supervisor must arrange work so the employee will be given a chance to apply new knowledge or skills while the material is still clear in his mind and interest is high. The trainee does not really know whether he has learned the material until he has been given a chance to apply it. If the material is not applied, it loses most of its value.

e. Evaluation
The purpose of all training is to promote learning. To determine whether the training has been a success or failure, the supervisor must evaluate this learning.
In the broadest sense, evaluation includes all the devices, methods, skills, and techniques used by the supervisor to keep himself and the employees informed as to their progress toward the objectives they are pursuing. The extent to which the employee has mastered the knowledge, skills, and abilities, or changed his attitudes, as determined by the program objectives, is the extent to which instruction has succeeded or failed.
Evaluation should not be confined to the end of the lesson, day, or program but should be used continuously. We shall note later the way this relates to the rest of the teaching process.

2. Teaching Methods
A teaching method is a pattern of identifiable student and instructor activity used in presenting training material.
All supervisors are faced with the problem of deciding which method should be used at a given time.

a. Lecture
The lecture is direct oral presentation of material by the supervisor. The present trend is to place less emphasis on the trainer's activity and more on that of the trainee.

b. Discussion
Teaching by discussion or conference involves using questions and other techniques to arouse interest and focus attention upon certain areas, and by doing so creating a learning situation. This can be one of the most

valuable methods because it gives the employees an opportunity to express their ideas and pool their knowledge.

    c. Demonstration
The demonstration is used to teach how something works or how to do something. It can be used to show a principle or what the results of a series of actions will be. A well-staged demonstration is particularly effective because it shows proper methods of performance in a realistic manner.

    d. Performance
Performance is one of the most fundamental of all learning techniques or teaching methods. The trainee may be able to tell how a specific operation should be performed but he cannot be sure he knows how to perform the operation until he has done so.
As with all methods, there are certain advantages and disadvantages to each method.

    e. Which Method to Use
Moreover, there are other methods and techniques of teaching. It is difficult to use any method without other methods entering into it. In any learning situation, a combination of methods is usually more effective than any one method alone.

Finally, evaluation must be integrated into the other aspects of the teaching-learning process.

It must be used in the motivation of the trainees; it must be used to assist in developing understanding during the training; and it must be related to employee application of the results of training.

This is distinctly the role of the supervisor.

BASIC FUNDAMENTALS OF SPORTS

CONTENTS

	Page
PRINCIPLES OF ATHLETICS	1
BASKETBALL	1
CROSS-COUNTRY AND DISTANCE RUNNING	4
SOCCER	8
SOFTBALL	11
SPEEDBALL	14
TOUCH FOOTBALL	18
VOLLEYBALL	23

BASIC FUNDAMENTALS OF SPORTS

PRINCIPLES OF ATHLETICS

ATHLETICS IN THE PHYSICAL TRAINING PROGRAM

- ❖ Athletics deserve a prominent place in the physical training program because they contribute to the increased efficiency of the student. Because of the competitive nature of athletics and their natural appeal, the students take part in them with enthusiasm. Athletic teams formed at the intramural and higher levels are a strong unifying influence and provide one of the best means of developing esprit de corps.

- ❖ The athletic sports selected must be vigorous to insure good conditioning value.

- ❖ All the components of physical fitness cannot be developed with athletics alone. These sports are beneficial primarily in sustaining interest in the program and maintaining a level of physical fitness. Therefore, athletics are to be considered as a supplement and not a substitute for the less interest conditioning drills.

BASKETBALL

INTRODUCTION
Basketball has enjoyed increased popularity and growth within the past few years, unequaled by any other American sport. It should be comparatively easy for an instructor to create interest in basketball among student personnel, both for conditioning and recreational purposes. Few sports have the potentialities that basketball has for developing coordination, endurance, skill, teamwork, and the will to win. It is an excellent activity for the sustaining stage. One of the objectives of a physical training program is 100 percent participation. A well-organized basketball program makes it possible to more nearly accomplish this objective than any other athletic activity.

BASIC SKILLS
Men prefer to play rather than practice so, whenever possible, a part of each instruction period should be devoted to a scrimmage game. To prevent the loss of program interest, the instructor should vary the practice routine, add new plays, organize tournaments, and devise other ways to maintain enthusiasm. He should use textbooks written by professional basketball coaches to plan and teach offensive and defensive plays.

    A. Fundamentals

        1. Shooting Baskets
           a. One-hand Set Shots: Shoot from a balanced position. Keep both feet on the floor. Follow through.
           b. Two-hand Set Shots: Shoot from a balanced position and apply equal pressure on the ball with each hand. Keep both feet on the floor. Follow through.

    c. Lay-ups: Jump high, reach high before releasing the ball. Spin the ball, using the backboard when possible.
    d. Shooting while on move. This is usually a one-handed shot. Shoot off opposite foot from the hand that releases the ball.
    e. Jump Shot: Jump high, release ball with one hand at apex of height. Most common shot today.
    f. Free Throws: These are one-hand and two-hand underhand throws and two-hand push shots. Put a slight back spin on the ball.

2. Ball-handling.
    a. Two-hand Chest Pass: Step in the direction of the pass. Use a wrist action to release the ball with a back spin.
    b. One-hand and Two-hand Bounce Pass: Step in the direction of the pass. Bounce the ball a reasonable distance in front of the receiver, putting a back spin on the ball with a wrist action.
    c. One-hand Baseball Pass: Step in the direction of the pass; throw as you would throw a baseball. This is used mostly for long passes.
    d. Two-hand Overhead Pass: Hold the ball above the head with the arms extended. Throw with a wrist action. This pass is used mainly to get the ball to the pivot man who is close to the basket.

3. Dribbling
    a. Changing Hand With Ball: Only one hand may touch the ball at one time while dribbling. The hand may be alternated.
    b. Change of Pace: Changing speed and direction while dribbling.
    c. Dribbling Exercise With Eyes Not Directly On Ball: Change direction; change hand; keep the head up with the eyes directed toward possible passing or shooting situations.

4. Footwork
    a. Pivoting: Give the pivotman or center special practice in pivoting. One foot remains stationary while the opposite foot is mobile.
    b. Individual Defense: Stress footwork and the position of the hands and body.
    c. Check Position of Feet When Shooting Various Types of Shots: Points to check: the position of balance; correct foot forward when in shooting position; the distance between each foot.

B. Small Group or Team Practice

1. Man-to-Man Defense
    a. Switching: Each defensive man is responsible for defending against a designated man, until a screen or block forces the defensive man to change defensive responsibility.
    b. Nonswitching: Each defensive man is responsible for a designated man with the defensive man going through or behind screens and blocks.

2. Man-to-man Offense: Various types of offensive formations have been especially designed to combat man-to-man defense. Use textbooks written by professional coaches for technical knowledge.

3. **Zone Defense:** There are numerous variations of this type defense aimed at defending a restricted area in front of the basket. The defensive target is the ball, not the man.

4. **Zone Offense:** The zone offense forces the defense to adjust position, as a unit, rapidly and often. Zone offense is most effective when employing rapid movement of the ball within the defense area.

5. **Defense Against Fast Break:** Stress rebound work on the offensive backboard. Stress court balance by offensive team.

6. **Fast Break Offense:** Move down court into scoring or offensive territory quickly.

PRACTICE DRILLS

Some practice routines are:

A. **Keep-Away:** Divide unit into two groups. Designate each individual's defensive responsibility by name or number. Use half of a basketball court as the playing area. The team in possession of the ball passes it among the team members until the defense gets possession of it. Basketball rules apply. Continue with each team taking turns as it gets possession of the ball.

B. **Shooting Exercise:** Divide unit into small groups. Each group has a ball. Designate the various positions on the floor where the shooting practice is to be done. Use a pre-arranged scoring method. Play numerous games, giving each group an opportunity to shoot from all positions on the floor.

C. **Dribbling Exercise:** Divide unit into two or three groups. Each group has a ball. Conduct a dribbling relay. Place obstacles for dribblers to avoid and designate the path each team will follow.

D. **Defense Exercises:** Use the two free throw circles and the restraining circle at center court. Place five men around the outside of each circle. One man is in the center of each ring. It is the job of the man in the center to intercept or deflect the path of the ball which is passed from man to man in the circle. When the man inside the circle succeeds in intercepting, deflecting, or touching the ball, the passer takes his place.

FACILITIES AND EQUIPMENT

A. **Facilities:** In some sections of the country, outdoor facilities may be used, and they are easily constructed. The minimum dimensions of a court for competition are approximately 74 feet by 42 feet; maximum dimensions are 94 feet by 50 feet.

B. **Equipment:** A basketball is the only required equipment. For highly organized competition, however, uniforms, special shoes, and other equipment may be required.

RULES

So-called college rules or, more correctly, The National Collegiate Athletic Association rules, are used in conducting basketball in the physical training program. Each year a new paper-bound guide booklet is published and sold by the NCAA.

CROSS-COUNTRY AND DISTANCE RUNNING

INTRODUCTION

    A. Long-distance running gives some benefits that cannot be obtained in the same degree from any other sport. It builds powerful leg muscles, increases the long capacity, and develops endurance. For these reasons, cross-country and distance running should be included in the physical training program. These sports require only a few miles of open space that is available at school. They do require time, however, and many physical training supervisors do not find it feasible to use them as individual full-time sports. Short cross-country runs and middle-distance runs can be used to supplement other activities, particularly the team sports or the sports that develop precision or agility rather than endurance. Short cross-country runs can be scheduled once a week, gradually increasing the distance as the physical condition of the men improves; or distance running can be combined with other activities such as the conditioning exercises.

    B. Cross-country and the distance runs do not enjoy equal popularity with other sports, for obvious reasons. They require great endurance, and endurance requires months of rigid training. There is a common belief that long-distance running is too strenuous, often resulting in permanent injury to the heart. While distance running may be harmful to the man who overdoses the sport, when he is not in proper physical condition, the conditioned, supervised distance runner is in no greater danger of strain than the man engaged in any other athletic activity.

LONG-DISTANCE RUNS

Any run over a mile is classified as a long-distance run. The instructor may vary the distance of the run during the season, or he may standardize it at whatever length will best suit his men or the facilities available to him. Two miles is the most popular distance. Often, the two-mile run is included as an event in track and field meets, but more frequently it is treated as a separate sport. The two-mile run may be run on any type of flat outdoor course, on a regular cinder track, or on a grass or dirt course. Because the ground is often frozen too hard for long-distance running during cold weather, the two-mile run is not recommended as a winter activity except in mild climates. The sport is too strenuous for very hot weather. The run cannot be held indoors. Constant pounding of the feet on the hard surface causes shin splints and injuries to the ankle joints.

CROSS-COUNTRY RUNS

Cross-country is a distance run held on a course laid out along roads, across fields, over hills, through woods, on any irregular ground. A flat cylinder or dirt track is not a suitable surface for cross-country running. Opinions vary as to the proper length of a cross-country course. Some runs are as long as six miles. Five miles used to be accepted as standard, but recently there has been a tendency to shorten the run to four or even three miles. Only if time is available for a full-season cross-country program should the physical training instructor try to train men for a five-mile course. If time is limited, or if cross-country running is being used to supplement other activities, the three-mile course is long enough for most men.

PLACE IN THE PROGRAM

Cross-country and distance running should be used only after the men reach the sustaining stage of conditioning. They should then be scheduled occasionally to provide variety in the program. Cross-country running has the advantage of allowing mass participation. Interest can be stimulated by putting the runs on a competitive basis.

BASIC SKILLS

A. Cross-Country Running Form: Running form in cross-country races varies with the terrain and the contour of the course. On the flat, use the same form as used in a two-mile run. The body lean should be between 5 and 10 percent. A lean of more than 10 percent places too much weight and strain on the legs. A lean of less than 5 percent is retarding. In running uphill, lean forward at a greater angle and cut the length of the stride. To gain an added lift, swing the arms high and bring the knees up high on each stride. Do not slow down after reaching the crest of the hill, but resume the flat course stride as soon as the ground levels off. The runner's stride will naturally lengthen in doing downhill, but he should not stretch his stride or increase his pace too much. There is less control and less balance when running downhill; therefore, there is greater danger of turning an ankle and of falling. Keep the arms low, swinging freely, and use them as a brake and as a balance. Coming onto the flat from a downhill run, do not slow down but float or coast into a flat course pace. More energy will be used in attempting to brake the speed of descent than in maintaining the faster pace and slowing down gradually. Run on the toes or the balls of the feet, rather than on the heels. Landing on the heels throughout a five-mile course would jolt the entire body injuriously. Runners who have a tendency to strike the heel on the ground should wear a cotton or sponge rubber pad in the heels of their shoes, unless their footgear has rubber heels.

B. Racing Tactics for Cross-Country

1. Teams can be pitted against each other in cross-country races. Certain members of the team may need encouragement along the way. If the team runs well-bunched for most of the course, the stronger runners can lead and encourage the weaker men. The pace should be scaled to the pace of the average runner on the team. Within a mile of the finish, however, the group should break and each man run out the race for himself.

2. If the coach prefers his team to run on an individual basis, there are several techniques for outwitting opponents. A good runner may not take the lead but stay behind an opponent and conserve his energy for the final sprint. The opponent may tire himself out trying to maintain the lead and become so discouraged when passed by a strong sprint near the finish line that he will not fight to reach the tape first. If leading an opponent, a runner may discourage him by constantly increasing the lead when he is out of sight. Opportunities for doing this frequently occur at corners of the course obscured by trees or bushes. If the leading runner sprints a short distance after rounding the corner, he may increase his lead 10 or 15 yards. After this has happened two or three times, an easily discouraged opponent may cease to be a serious contender for the race.

PRACTICE METHODS

A. Conditioning is more essential to distance and cross-country running than to any other sport. Championship distance running depends on stamina, and stamina can be developed only through constant training. A man of only average ability can become an outstanding distance runner by steady and careful training. Hiking is the best method for getting into condition before the season opens. Long walks build up leg muscles. During the first month of the season, training should be gradual, starting with short distances and increasing day by day. At first, the legs will become stiff, but the stiffness gradually disappears if running is practiced for a while every day. To prevent strain, it is essential to limber up thoroughly each day before running.

B. In the mass training of a large group, leaders should be stationed at the head and the rear of the column, and they should make every effort to keep the men together. After determining the abilities of the men in cross-country running, it is advisable to divide the unit into three groups. The poorest conditioned group is started first, the best conditioned group last. The starting time of the groups should be staggered so that all of them come in about the same time. In preliminary training, the running is similar to ordinary road work in that it begins with rather slow jogging, alternating with walking. The speed and distance of the run is gradually increased. As the condition of the men improves, occasional sprints may be introduced. At first, the distance run is from one-half to one mile. It is gradually increased to two or three miles. On completing the run, the men should be required to continue walking for three or four minutes before stopping, to permit a gradual cooling off and return to normal physiological functioning.

FACILITIES AND EQUIPMENT

A. A course three or five miles long should be measured and marked by one or the three methods specified below:

1. Directional arrows fastened to the top of a tall post and placed at every point where the course turns. Such signs should also be placed at ever other point where there may be doubt as to the direction of travel.

2. A lime line placed on the ground over the entire course.

3. Flags: they should be clearly visible to the runners.
   a. A red flag indicates a left turn.
   b. A white flag indicates a right turn.
   c. A blue flag indicates the course is straight ahead.

B. There should be at least one stopwatch (preferably three) for timing the runners.

RULES

A. Team Members: A cross-country team shall consist of seven men, unless otherwise agreed. In dual meets, a maximum of twelve men may be entered, but a maximum of seven shall enter into the scoring.

B. Scoring: First place shall score 1 point, second place 2, third place 3, and so on. All men who finish the course shall be ranked and tallied in this manner. The team score shall then be determined by totaling the points scored by the first five men of each team to finish. The team scoring the least number of points shall be the winner. Note: Although the sixth and seventh runners of a team to finish do not score points toward their team's total, it should be noted that their places, if better than those of any of the first five of an opposing team, serve to increase the team score of the opponents.

C. Cancellation of Points: If less than five (or the number determined prior to the race) finish, the places of all members of that team shall be disregarded.

D. Tie Event: In case the total points scored by two or more teams result in a tie, the event shall be called a tie.

SOCCER

INTRODUCTION

A. Soccer is one of the best athletic activities for developing endurance, agility, leg strength, and a great degree of skill in using the legs. The game is the most popular sport in Europe and is the national game of many of the Central and South American countries. In recent years, it has become popular in United States schools and colleges.

B. A soccer ball is the only equipment needed for the game, and the men can learn to play it easily. The men do not need much skill to participate, but the amount they can developed in unlimited.

PLACE IN THE PROGRAM

Soccer should be introduced into the physical training program during the latter part of the slow improvement stage and used as a competitive activity in the sustaining stage. It is primarily a spring or fall sport. Any level field is suitable for competition. The boundaries for the soccer field are similar to the dimensions for a football field. Goal posts are essential to the game, but they are easily constructed and are usually of a temporary nature, so that they may be removed when not in use.

BASIC SKILLS

A. Passing: Passing with the feet is the basic means of moving the ball. Short passes are easier to control and can be done more accurately than long ones. Emphasis should be continually placed on skill in passing.

B. Dribbling: The ball is dribbled by a series of kicks with the inside or outside of the foot. Do not kick with the toe. Keep the head over the ball when kicking and propel it only a short distance at a time. Keep it close to the feet. When the ball gets very far from the feet while dribbling, an opposing player can easily take it away.

C. Instep Kicking: The instep kick, which is the basic soccer kick, is made from the knee joint instead of from the hip as in football. The toe does not come in contact with the ball. It is pointed downward and the instep (the shoe laces) is applied to the ball with a vigorous snap from the knee. For a stationary ball, the non-kicking foot is alongside the ball at the time of the kick. For a ball rolling toward the kicker, his non-kicking foot stops short of the ball; for a ball rolling away from the kicker, his non-kicking foot stops beyond the ball. The kicker must keep his eye on the ball until it has left his foot.

D. Inside-of-the-Foot Kicking: The ball is kicked with the inside of the foot and the leg is swung from the hip. The toe is turned outward and the sole of the foot is parallel with the ground as the foot strikes the ball. The tall should be well under the body at the time of contact. This kick is used for short passes and for dribbling.

E. Foot Trapping: The foot trap is the method of stopping the ball by trapping it between the ground and the foot. Place the sole of the foot on top of the ball at the instant it touches the ground, but do not stamp on it. Keep the foot relaxed. This is an effective way to stop a high-flying ball.

F. Shin Trapping: The shin trap is a method of stopping the ball with the shins. Stand just forward of the spot where the ball should strike the ground and allow it to strike the shins in flight or on the bounce. Use either one or both legs from the knee down, but do not allow the ball to strike the toe.

G. Body Trapping: The body trap is another method of gaining control of a ball in flight. Intercept the ball with any part of the upper body except the arms and hands. Keep the body relaxed and inclined toward the ball. To keep the ball from bouncing, move backward from it as it strikes the body. This will drop the ball at the feet in position for dribbling or passing.

H. Heading: Heading is the technique for changing the direction of the flight of a ball by butting it with the head. Tense the neck muscles and jump up to meet the ball. Butt the ball with the forehead at about the hairline to reverse its direction; use the side of the head to deflect it to the side. Always watch the ball, even during contact.

OFFENSIVE AND DEFENSIVE POSITIONS

The forwards usually play on the offensive half of the field and remain in a W formation. The fullbacks usually play on the defensive half of the field. The halfbacks are the backbone of the team; they move forward on the offense and back on defense. The goal keeper almost always remains within a few feet of the goal.

DRILLS TO DEVELOP BASIC SKILLS

Several skills are recommended to develop skill in kicking, passing, and shooting. The circle formation may be used for training in any of the basic skills. The ball may be headed or trapped as it is moved around or across the circle.

ABRIDGED RULES

A. A soccer team is composed of eleven players.

B. The player propels the ball by kicking it with the feet or any part of the legs, by butting it with his head, and by hitting it with any portion of his body except his arms or hands.

C. The goalkeeper is the only man allowed to use his hands on the ball, but he may only handle the ball in the goalkeeper's area. The term hands includes the whole arm from the point of the shoulder down.

D. A goal is made by causing the ball to cross completely the section of the goal line lying between the uprights and under the cross bar.

E. Each goal scores one point for the team scoring the goal.

F. The penalty for a foul committed anywhere on the playing field (except by the defensive team in its penalty area) is a free kick awarded to the team that committed the foul.

G. All opponents must be at least 10 yards from the ball when a free kick is taken.

10

H. The penalty for a foul committed by the defensive team in its penalty area is a penalty kick.

I. A penalty kick is a free kick at the goal from the spot 12 yards directly in front of the goal. The only players allowed within the penalty area at the time of the kick are the kicker and the defending goalkeeper.

J. An official game consists of four quarters.

K. Teams change goals at the end of every quarter.

L. In the event of a tie, an extra quarter is played.

M. After a ball has crossed a side line and has been declared out of play, it is put back into play by a free kick from the side line by a member of the team opposing the team that caused the ball to be out of bounds. The kick is taken from the point at which the ball crosses the side line as it goes out of bounds.

N. When the offensive team causes the ball to go behind the opposing team's goal line, excluding the portion between the goal posts, the opposing team is awarded a goal kick—a free kick taken within the goal area that must come out of the penalty area to be in play.

O. When the defensive team causes the ball to go behind its own goal line, excluding the portion between the goal posts, the opposing team is awarded a corner kick—a free kick taken by a member of the offensive team at the quarter circle at the corner flag-post nearest to where the ball went behind the goal line. The flat-post must not be removed.

P. The game is started and, after a goal has been scored, is resumed by placing the ball in the center of the mid-field line. Players must be on their side of the line until the ball is kicked. The ball must be kicked forward and must move a least two feet to be legal. The first kicker may not touch the ball twice in succession at the kick-off. The opposing team must be ten yards from the ball until it moves.

SOFTBALL

INTRODUCTION

A. Softball is a game that is known in every corner of the country and has become a familiar sight in every sandlot in America. During and since World War II, it has become one of the principal physical training activities.

B. Softball is patterned after baseball, but has different advantages because it requires less equipment and is easily adapted to every age group. It requires a smaller play area; the ball is larger and softer; and the bats are lighter, making them easier to handle. Because of its popularity, a majority of our young people have a general understanding of softball and softball rules, but only a comparative few possess the skill and knowledge to obtain the maximum benefit and satisfaction from the game

PLACE IN THE PROGRAM

A. Softball is a sustaining type of activity. It does not require continuous exertion on the part of each player; however, it is an enjoyable and occasionally strenuous game that should be included in the physical training program.

B. When a group already knows something about pitching, fielding, and batting, the instructor should give only a brief review of these fundamental skills, but place more emphasis on the rules and offensive and defensive strategy. Most of the time devoted to softball should be used for organized competition.

ORGANIZATION OF INSTRUCTION

When instruction is given on the basic skills and techniques, the students should first be shown the correct method of executing each skill. The class should then be divided into groups to practice. Ample time should be provided to familiarize each individual with the technique of playing each position as well as the basic skills necessary to play every position. When this instruction is completed, the class should be divided into teams for organized competition.

BASIC SKILLS

A. Batting: Select a bat that balances easily—hands grasp the handle at a point where the butt is neither too heavy nor too light. For a right-handed batter, the left foot points at about a 45° angle toward the pitcher, and the right foot points toward homeplate. The feet are about 8 inches apart. The head and eyes face the pitcher, and the bat is over the right shoulder, hands away from the body. The batting position is slightly to the rear of the center of the plate. In swinging, keep the eyes on the ball, twisting at the waist. As a result of the twist, the arms will swing automatically. The power of the swing is developed with a snap of the wrists and the extension of the arms in the follow-through.

B. Bunting: The stance for bunting is the same as for batting. When the ball leaves the pitcher's hand, immediately bring the bat from over the shoulder, moving the right hand slightly up the handle, until the bat is directly over the plate. Rotate the body so that it faces the pitcher. The feet are comfortably apart. Meet the ball squarely, absorbing the shock with the arms. Hold the edge of the bat perpendicular to the direction in which the ball is to be bunted.

C. Base Running: Upon hitting the ball, the runner must start quickly without watching where the ball goes. He should get to the first base as fast as possible and be ready to continue running at the coach's direction. Speed is the most important factor, but running the shortest distance between bases is also essential.

D. Sliding: Use the hook slide going into the base, with the body relaxed, extending either foot in a sweeping motion, touching the toe to the bag.

E. Catching: Assume the knee bend position, with the upper arms parallel to the ground, forearms vertical and palms down. As the ball strikes the mitt, grasp it with the bare hand. On high pitches, cup the fingers of the bare hand to prevent injury. On low pitches, extend the palms toward the pitcher with the thumbs down. Always avoid pointing the fingers toward the pitcher. The catcher must not sacrifice accuracy for speed in throwing to bases and must learn through experience when he can throw a player out at base.

F. Pitching: Pitching, to a large degree, determines a team's defensive strength, and pitching can only be developed through practice. To hold the ball, grasp it loosely with the fingers, the index, middle, and third finger on one side and the thumb and fourth finger on the other side. The most effective manner of pitching is the windmill pitch. To start the wind-up, face the homeplate with both feet on the rubber. The ball is held in front with both hands. Raise the left foot to the rear as the right arm swings backward. The body pivots to the right, the left hand is extended and balances the motion, and the head and eyes remain on the catcher's glove. When the right arm reaches the nine o'clock position, step forward with the left foot directly toward homeplate, swing the arm forward, and twist the body to the left. With a snap of the wrist on the underhand swing, release the ball and follow through. Control is very important and must be gained through practice.

G. Infield Playing: An infielder must anticipate at all times what he should do in case he has to play the ball. On batted ground balls, he should play the ball to his front. Field each ground ball with the feet apart, hands well out in front. When the ball strikes the glove, secure it with the bare hand. The hands and arms should relax, and the arms should be drawn backward toward the right hip preparatory to the throw.

H. Outfield Playing: An outfielder should be alert and fast and able to judge the ball so he can get in the best position to catch it. It takes practice to become a successful fielder. To catch a fly ball, he extends the arms forward, forming a cup with the hands. He keeps his eyes on the ball until he has firm possession of it. He catches ground balls in the same way as the infielder (see G above).

DRILLS

A. Pitching and Catching: Divide the class into two lines fifty feet apart; one side will pitch, the other will catch. Make corrections on form for both pitching and catching. emphasize form and control. Change over.

B. Infield Play: Divide the class into seven-man groups. Place each group in a separate area, simulating (if necessary) the softball diamond. Designate a first, second, and third baseman, and a shortstop. Choose one man to hit balls and one to catch at homeplate. The player who hits balls first calls a play such as first base, double play, throw it home, etc. He then hits a ground ball to one of the infielders who, in turn, carries out the prescribed play. Demand enthusiasm and hustle. Change over occasionally and allow each man to play each position.

C. Outfield Play: Place seven men in the outfield, but do not designate definite positions. Have a player hit both fly and ground balls to the field. Use one player to catch balls at homeplate. After each ball has been played, have it relayed back to the hitter. Change positions so that each player has an opportunity to play in the outfield.

D. Base Running: Divide the class into fifteen-man groups. Time each runner in a complete circuit of bases. Stimulate competition. Critique each runner.

E. Hitting and Bunting: Divide the class into regular nine-man teams. Place one team in the infield to shag balls. The players on the other team take turns at bat, hitting ten balls each. On the last pitch, they lay down a bunt and run to first base, trying to beat the throw. Change over.

OFFENSIVE AND DEFENSIVE STRATEGY

A. Offensive: Hit only good balls (balls in the strike zone). Runners should run out fly balls at top speed, in case the ball is dropped or an error is committed. There is a better possibility of stealing a base than of the next batter hitting safely. Do not hesitate in stealing. Do not attempt to steal third base when two men are out, because a runner should be able to score from second base on a hit or on an error. It is best to attempt to steal second base with two outs. With no outs and runners on first and second base, a bunt combined with a double steal is good strategy. A runner can usually score from third base on a fly ball or on an error.

B. Defensive: A play should always back up another player receiving a throw at a base, or a player attempting to make a play on a fly or ground ball. The player who is nearest the ball should call for it and make the catch or play. Each player should be aware of the situation and know exactly what to do if he receives the ball. Receive bunts, flys, and ground balls with both hands. Have firm possession of the ball before attempting a throw. On force plays, do not stand on the base. It is better to make certain of one out, rather than risk an error in trying for a double play. When a shorter throw can put a runner out at base, it is best to attempt the shorter throw. With runners on first and second base, it is better to force out at third than to try a double play from second to first base. An outfielder should throw the ball directly to the spot where the play is likely to be made, unless it is a long fly and a relay appears to be quicker.

SPEEDBALL

INTRODUCTION AND GENERAL DESCRIPTION

Speedball is a game that offers vigorous and varied action with plenty of scoring opportunities. It is easy to learn and provides spontaneous fun. Little equipment is needed—a ball is all that is absolutely necessary. Speedball combines the kicking, trapping, and intercepting elements of soccer; the passing game of basketball; and the punting, drop-kicking, and scoring pass of football. Two teams of eleven men each play the game under official rules, but any number of players may successfully constitute a team. An inflated leather ball, usually a soccer ball, is used. The playing field is a football field with a football goal post at each end. The game starts with a soccer-type kickoff. The kicking team tries to retain possession of the ball and advance it toward the opposite goal by passing or kicking it. Running with the ball is not allowed, so there is no tackling or interference. When the ball touches the ground, it cannot be picked up with the hands or caught on the bounce, but must be played as in soccer until it is raised into the air directly from a kick; then the hands are again eligible for use. When the ball goes out of bounds over the side lines, it is given to a player of the team opposite that forcing the ball out, and is put into play with a basketball throw-in; when it goes over the end line without a score, it is given to a player of the opposing team who may either pass or kick it onto the field. When two opposing players are contesting the possession of a held ball, the official tosses the ball up between them as in basketball. Points are scored by kicking the ball under the crossbar of the goal posts, drop-kicking the ball over the crossbar, completing a forward pass into the end zone for a touchdown, or by kicking the ball under the crossbar of the goal posts on a penalty kick.

PLACE IN THE PROGRAM

Speedball, like soccer, should be introduced into the physical training program during the latter part of the toughening stage and used as a competitive activity in the sustaining stage. It may be played any time the weather permits, but it is primarily a spring or fall activity.

BASIC SKILLS

A. Soccer Techniques
   1. Kicking
   2. Passing
   3. Heading
   4. Trapping

B. Football Techniques
   1. Punting
   2. Drop-kicking
   3. Forward passing

C. Basketball Techniques
   1. Passing
   2. Receiving
   3. Pivoting

D. Kickups and Lifts: The kickup is a play in which the player lifts the ball into the air with his feet so that he may legally play the ball with his hands. The kickup is generally used to make the transition from ground play to aerial play. The technique of making the play depends upon whether the ball is rolling or stationary. To kick up a ball rolling or bouncing toward the player, the foot is held on the ground with the toe drawn down until the ball rolls onto the foot, then the foot is raised, projecting the ball upward. If the ball is stationary, the player rolls it backward with one foot, then places the foot where the ball will roll onto it. He can then lift the ball with that foot. If a ball is running away from the player, he should stop it with a foot and play it as a stationary ball. There is also a method of raising the ball by standing over it with a foot on either side. He presses his feet against the ball and jumps into the air, propelling the ball into his hands.

OFFENSIVE POSITIONS AND STRATEGY

The positions of the players in speedball are much the same as in soccer. However, some of the positions are designated by different names. There are eleven players on each team. The forward line is composed of five players: the right end, right forward, center, left forward, and left end. The second line consists of right halfback, fullback, and left halfback. In the next line is the right guard and left guard. The player who defends the goal is the goal guard. The strategy employed in speedball during offensive play is very similar to that of soccer.

DEFENSIVE PLAY

There are two types of defensive formations in speedball: man-for-man and position defense. Man-for-man defense is recommended for beginning players.

ABRIDGED RULES

A. The Field: 360 feet long and 160 feet wide (a regulation football field).

B. Players: Eleven on a team. The goal guard has no special privileges.

C. Time: Ten-minute quarters, two minutes between. Ten minutes between halves. Five minutes for extra overtime periods. (Begin first overtime by a jump ball (see G.3. below) at center, same goals; change goals in the event of a second overtime period.)

D. Winner of Toss: The winner of the toss has the choice of kicking, receiving, or defending a specific goal.

E. Starting Second and Fourth Quarters: The ball is given to the team that had possession at the end of the previous quarter, out of bounds, as in basketball.

F. Half: The team that received at the start of the first half kicks off at the beginning of the second half.

G. The Game: The game is started with a kickoff from the middle line (50-yard line), both teams being required to remain back of their respective restraining lines until the ball is kicked. The ball must travel forward.

1. The most characteristic feature of the playing rules of speedball is the differentiation between a fly ball (or aerial ball) and a ground ball. A player is not permitted to touch a ground ball with his hands and must play it as in soccer. A fly ball is one that has risen into the air directly from the foot of a player (example: punt, drop-kick, place-kick, or kickup). Such a ball may be caught with the hands

provided the catch is made before the ball strikes the ground again. A kickup is a ball that is so kicked by a player that he can catch it himself. A bounce from the ground may not be touched with the hand because it has touched the ground since being kicked. This rule prohibits thee ordinary basketball dribble, but one overhead dribble (throwing the ball into the air and advancing to catch it before it hits the ground) is permitted.

2. If a team causes the ball to go out of bounds over the side lines, a free thrown-in (any style) is given to the opposing team. When the ball goes over the end line without scoring, it is given to the opponents who may pass or kick from out of bounds at that point.

3. In case two players are contesting the possession of a held ball, even in the end zone, a tie ball is declared and the ball is tossed up between them.

4. The kick-off is made from any place on or behind the 50-yard line. Team A (the kicking team) must be behind the ball when it is kicked. Team B must stay back of its restraining line (ten yards' distance) until the ball is kicked (penalty—a violation). The ball must go forward before A may play it (penalty—violation). Kick off out of bounds to opponents at that spot. A kick-off touched by B and going out of bounds, no impetus added, still belongs to B. A kick-off, in possession and control of B and then fumbled out of bounds, belongs to A at that spot. A field goal from kick-off (under crossbar, etc.) scores 3 points.

H. Scoring Methods

1. Field Goal (3 points): A soccer-type kick, in which a ground ball is kicked under the crossbar and between the goal posts from the field of play or end zone. (A punt going straight through is not a field goal for it is not a ground ball. The ball must hit the ground first.). A drop-kick from the field of play that goes under a crossbar does not count as a field goal. A drop-kick from the end zone that goes under the crossbar counts as a field goal; if it goes over the crossbar, it is ruled as a touch back.

2. Drop-kick (2 points): A scoring drop-kick must be made from the field of play and go over the crossbar and between the uprights. The ball must hit the ground before it is kicked (usually with the instep).

3. End Goal (1 point): This is a ground ball which receives its impetus (kicked or legally propelled by the body) from any player, offensive or defensive, in the end zone and passes over the end line but not between the goal posts.

4. Penalty Kick (1 point): This is a ball kicked from the penalty mark that goes between the goal posts and under the crossbar. The penalty mark is placed directly in front of the goal at the center of the goal line.

5. Touchdown (1 point): A touchdown is a forward pass from the field of play completed in the end zone. The player must be entirely in the end zone. If he is on the goal line or has one foot in the field of play and the other in the end zone, the ball is declared out of bounds. If a forward pass is missed, the ball continues in

play but must be returned to the field of play before another forward pass or drop-kick may be made.

I. Substitutions: Substitutions may be made any time when the ball is not in play. If a player is withdrawn, he may not return during that same period.

J. Time Out: Three legal time-outs of two minutes each are permitted each team during the game.

K. Fouls

   1. Personal (four disqualify): Kicking, tripping, charging, pushing, holding, blocking, or unnecessary roughness of any kind, such as running into an opponent from behind. Kicking at a fly ball and thereby kicking an opponent.

   2. Technical: Illegal substitution, more than three time-outs in a game, unsportsmanlike conduct, unnecessarily delaying the game.

   3. Violation: Traveling with the ball, touching a ground ball with the hands or arms, double overhead dribble, violating tie ball, and kicking or kneeing a fly ball before catching it.

   4. Penalties: (The offended player shall attempt the kick.)

	Penalty	Location
Personal	In field of play	1 kick with no follow-up
Technical	In field of play	1 kick with no follow-up
Violation	In field of play	Out of bounds to opponent
Personal	In end zone	2 kick with no follow-up on last kick
Technical	In end zone	1 kick with no follow-up
Violation	In end zone	1 kick with no follow-up

I. Summary of Fouls

   1. Fouls in the field of play allow no follow-up while fouls in the end zone always allow follow-up.

   2. On penalty kicks, with no follow-up, only the kicker and goalie are involved.

   3. On penalty kicks, with a follow-up, the kicking side is behind the ball and the defending side behind the end line or in the field of play. No one is allowed in the end zone or between the goal post except the goal guard. The kicker cannot play the ball again until after another player plays it, and he must make an actual attempt at goal.

TOUCH FOOTBALL

INTRODUCTION

Touch football has become a major active game on the lower levels of competition. Considering its similarity to football and yet its comparative simplicity, it is easy to understand the popularity of the game. The modification of regulation football rules for touch football eliminates the necessity for much special equipment, training, and professional leadership. Touch football encourages participation, reduces the number of injuries, and simplifies the teaching of fundamental rules, techniques, and skills.

PLACE IN THE PROGRAM

Touch football is an excellent conditioning activity, and it should be included in both the physical training and intramural programs. It may be used in the latter part of the toughening stage and during the sustaining stage of physical conditioning. It should be played in the fall when the interest in football is at its peak. Any level field can be used. Goal posts are desirable but not absolutely necessary.

ORGANIZATION OF INSTRUCTION

Most men know something about football, but not all have had an opportunity to play. Several short periods should be devoted to the instruction of all men in the basic fundamentals. A desirable method is to give five to ten minutes of instruction at the beginning of each football period and follow it by actual play.

BASIC SKILLS

A. Offensive Stance: Touch football emphasizes speed; therefore, a high offensive stance should be used to facilitate a fast getaway. The feet should be about shoulder width apart and parallel, knees bent, thighs just above the horizontal and back nearly parallel with the ground. The head and eyes are up, and the right hand is extended straight downward, the fingers curled under, the thumb toward the rear. The left arm rests on the left thigh. There are many variations of this basic stance that may be used. The general principles are: Keep the feet spread for balance, the body under control, and the head up with the eyes on an opponent or the ball.

B. Defensive Stance: This type stance may be similar to the offensive stance or somewhat higher to allow for better visibility and free use of the hands to ward off blockers. The same principles of balance, body control, and vision used in the offensive stance are applicable to the defensive stance.

C. Blocking: Touch football rules do not permit the blocker to have both feet off the ground at the same time (flying block); therefore, the blocker should maintain a wide base for shoulder, upright, or cross-body blocks. For the shoulder block, the hands should be close to the chest, the elbows raised sideward, the feet under the body and widely spread, the head up, and the buttocks low. Upon contact, the feet should be moved rapidly in short, choppy steps to force the body forward, thus keeping the shoulder in contact with the opponent. The upright block is useful in the open field and is executed by the player while standing nearly erect. The feet are widely spread, knees slightly bent, the trunk inclined slightly forward, and the head erect. The arms are raised, and the hands are placed on the chest, forearms forward to contact the opponent. Due to the nature of the block, the opponent is contacted above the waist.

In performing the cross-body block, the blocker uses the hip to contact the opponent, usually in the area of the thighs. The execution of this type of block requires the blocker to throw his head, shoulders, and arms past the target area, thus bringing his hip into contact with his opponent. Then, assisted by movement of the hands and feet which are in contact with the ground, he forces the opponent backward or down. The shoulder, upright, or cross-body blocks may be used in the line or in the open field.

D. Ball Carrying: The first point to stress in ball carrying is the grip of the ball. The ball is placed in the arm with its long axis parallel to the forearm. It is held firmly and close to the body. The hand grips the lower point of the ball with the fingers spread to form a firm grip. It is difficult to teach the fine points of ball carrying in a few hours of instruction. Stress the principles. Teach runners to carry the ball in the arm away from the opponent. The runner should be cautioned to follow his interference and to keep his head up so he can avoid his opponents.

E. Forward Passing: Forward passing is one of the principal means of advancing the ball in touch football. Teach the method of gripping or holding the ball with the fingers spread on the laces and toward the end of the ball, cocking the arm with the hand holding the ball close to the head and the wrist rotated so that the rear point of the ball is pointing toward the head. The ball is delivered with a baseball catcher's peg motion, by extending the arm and imparting a spiral to the ball. To make a successful forward pass, it is usually best for the passer to have the feet spread comfortably and in contact with the ground, the free hand extended to aid the balance. He throws the ball to a spot where the receiver can catch it without breaking his stride. Do not allow beginners to attempt jump passes, as the successful throwing of this type of pass requires the skill of an experienced forward passer.

F. Pass Receiving: To catch a forward pass requires the receiver to keep his eyes on the ball, to run to the spot where he can reach the ball, to catch it without breaking stride, and to take it out of the air by relaxing the hands as the ball strikes. In receiving a pass over the shoulder, the little fingers are facing, with the thumbs outward and all fingers spread. In catching a pass while facing the passer, the receiver should catch a high pass with the thumbs facing and the little fingers out; and a low pass with the little fingers facing and the thumbs pointing outward.

DRILLS TO DEVELOP FUNDAMENTALS

It is recommended that the time available for instruction in the fundamentals be used in teaching the following skills: stance, shoulder block, cross-body block, forward passing, and pass receiving.

A. Stance Drill: Use the extended rectangular formation. Demonstrate the stance and tell the men they will execute the drill by the numbers. At the count of one, place the feet in position. At the count of two, bend the knees and trunk. At the count of three, lean forward and place one hand on the ground. After checking for errors and making corrections, command "UP" and execute the drill again. Have the men do this several times before progressing to the next drill.

B. Blocking Drills: All the blocks may be practiced by forming the class into two lines facing one another and having the men pair off. Explain the drill, demonstrate the block desired, and designate one line as blockers and the other as opponents. After several practice blocks, have the blockers become the opponents and the opponents become the blockers. During the course of the drill, emphasize the three phases of blocking: the approach, contact, and follow-through.

C. Forward Passing Drill: Form the class in groups of ten men each. The groups form two lines with the men about ten feet apart and the two lines ten to fifteen yards apart. Using at least one ball to a group, practice grip, balance, throwing with a spiral, and follow-through. The ball is thrown by each man, in turn, to the next man in the opposite line who catches it and throws.

D. Passing and Receiving Drill: Each of the groups is formed as for the drill outlined in C above. One man, the center, is stationed between the two files with the ball. One file is designated as passers and the other as receivers. The center snaps the ball to the first passer. He passes to the first receiver who runs down the field at the snap of the ball. The receiver catches the pass and returns the ball to the center. Upon his return, the receiver joins the "passer" file and the passer joins the "receiver" file. This rotation continues until all men have an opportunity to throw and receive forward passes.

E. Other Drills: If time permits, other fundamental drills may be included, such as snapping the ball from center, kicking, lateral passing, and other individual skills of a specialty nature.

OFFENSIVE FORMATIONS AND PLAY

A. A nine-man team is recommended. Three offensive formations are suggested for this size team. Of the three formations suggested, the double wing-back is the best.

B. To complete the instruction in offensive play, it will be necessary to insure that some member of the team can perform the individual specialties. These special skills are passing the ball from center, punting, free kicking for kick-offs, backfield pivots, handoffs, etc.

C. Men like to develop their own plays and should be encouraged to do so. Time must be made available for them to practice such plays before using them in a game.

DEFENSIVE PLAY

The class should be shown several defensive formations. Four different ones are applicable for the nine-man team. The selection of a defense depends upon the opponent's offense. The 4-2-2-1 and the 5-1-2-1 are better pass defense formations than the 4-3-2 and the 5-2-2. The latter formations are weak "down the middle." However, the 4-3-2 and 5-2-2 are stronger against a running attack. If fewer men are employed on a team, the defense could be altered by eliminating either linemen or backs, as required.

ORGANIZATION AND ADMINISTRATION

A. The instructor may divide the class into teams from the roster or by selecting team captains who, in turn, choose the remaining members of their teams.

B. The officials may be assistant instructors or selected individuals from the class. It is suggested that there should be at least one official for each game that is played.

Close supervision of play and strict enforcement of rules are necessary to prevent injuries from excessive roughness.

C. To insure the success of touch football in a physical training period, the teams should be organized into a class league to stimulate interest and competition, and to select the championship team.

D. There should be one ball for each fifteen men.

E. The area for practice and play should be grassed and level. The field should conform as nearly as possible to the size specified in paragraph 9.A.1.

RULES

It is important that the participants know the rules that govern touch football. It increases the players' enjoyment in the activity, lessens the chance of injury, and results in an organized contest. Official National Collegiate Athletic Association football rules shall govern all play except those special rules pertinent to touch football, as stated in the following subparagraphs.

A. Rule I: Field and Equipment
  1. Section 1 – Field: The game shall be played on a regulation football field with goal posts. When space is limited, the dimensions of the field may be reduced to 300 feet long by 120 feet wide.
  2. Section 2 – Uniforms: Distinctive jerseys, shorts, sweat suits, or trousers, and basketball shoes or regulation footwear may be worn. Pads, helmets, and cleated shoes are not authorized.

B. Rule II: Length of Game
  1. Section 1 – Periods: The game shall be played in four periods each ten minutes in length, with a one-minute interval between the first and second and the third and fourth periods; and with a ten-minute interval between the second and third periods.

  2. Section 2 – Contest: By mutual agreement of opposing coaches or captains, before the start of contest, the length of the periods may be shortened or lengthened.

  3. Section 3 – Time Out: Time out shall be taken
      a. After a touchdown, field goal, safety, or touch back.
      b. During a try for a point.
      c. After an incomplete forward pass.
      d. When the ball goes out of bounds.
      e. During the enforcement or declination of penalties.

C. Rule III: Players and Substitutes

  1. Section 1 – Players (nine-man team): Each team shall consist of nine players. The offensive team shall have a minimum of five players on the scrimmage line when the ball is snapped. Note: The following diagram designates the position of the players:

```
           END    GUARD        CENTER         GUARD    END
                            QUARTERBACK
                          HALFBACK   HALFBACK
                               FULLBACK
```

2. Section 2 – Players (six-man game): Each team shall consist of six players. The offensive team shall have a minimum of three players on the scrimmage line when the ball is snapped. Note: The following diagram designates the position of the players.

```
             END           CENTER          END
                   HALFBACK    HALFBACK
                         FULLBACK
```

3. Section 3 – Substitutions: Unrestricted substitutions may be made when
   a. The ball is dead.
   b. The clock is running, provided substitutions are completed and the ball is snapped within 25 seconds after the ball is ready for play.

D. Rule IV: Playing Regulations

1. Section 1: Starting the game and putting ball in play after any score shall be as prescribed by the NCAA Football Rule Book, with exception of Rule 4, Sections 2 and 3.
2. Section 2 – Kick-off: The receiving team, in a nine-man game, shall have three players within five yards of its own restraining line until the ball is kicked.
3. Section 3 – Restriction: In a six-man game, the only restriction on the receiving team is that all players must remain back of their own restraining line until the ball is kicked.
4. Section 4 – Fumbled Ball: A ball that is fumbled and touches the ground during a run, kick, or lateral pass play, may not be advanced by either team. The ball may be touched and recovered by any player. It shall be dead and in possession of the player who first touches it after it strikes the ground.
   Note: Players shall be warned against diving on fumbled balls and may be penalized for unnecessary roughness.
5. Section 5 – Fumbled Ball or Lateral Pass: A fumbled ball or lateral pass, intercepted or recovered before it touches the ground, may be advanced by any player.
6. Section 6 – Downed Ball By Legal Touch: The player in possession of the ball is downed and the ball is dead when such player is touched by an opponent with both hands simultaneously above the waist and below the head.
7. Section 7 – Forward Passing: One forward pass may be made during each scrimmage play from behind the passer's scrimmage line.
8. Section 8 – Eligible Receivers: All players of offensive and defensive teams are eligible to receive forward passes. Two or more receives may successively touch a forward pass.

E. Rule V – Fouls and Penalties. Section 1 – Use of hands and arms. For both offense and defense, as prescribed in NCAA Football Rule Book.

23

VOLLEYBALL

INTRODUCTION

    A. Volleyball is a popular sport. The game entails much physical activity, yet it is not strenuous. It is, therefore, a game for young and older men alike, for beginners and for skilled players. It may be played indoors or outdoors on any type of terrain. As an informal activity, volleyball can be played by any number of men; as an organized activity, it provides, as few other sports do, a game for twelve men to play in a limited area.

    B. While volleyball requires no great skill to play, it does permit a high degree of proficiency. A man naturally gets more enjoyment when he knows the game and plays it well. For this reason, instruction in the basic skills should be provided.

ORGANIZATION

Usually a ten- to fifteen-minute period of instruction, followed by scrimmage during the first three or four classes is enough to teach the basic skills, rules, and techniques of volleyball. More time can be given to teaching basic skills, if available, but the emphasis is on competitive play rather than on formal instruction. It is best to lecture and demonstrate to the entire class, then divide the class into smaller groups for practice. For drills and scrimmages, divide the class so that there will be from twelve to twenty-four men to each court. One court may be used for instruction by allowing twelve players at a time to execute the drill while the other class members observe, act as coaches, or retrieve balls. After the instruction phase of training has been completed, divide the class into six-man teams. Organize the teams on the basis of ability. All teams should be as nearly equal as possible.

PLACE IN THE PROGRAM

Volleyball may be used occasionally as a competitive activity during the sustaining stage. It is a year-round sport, but it should be included in the physical training program only when it is impractical to conduct a more strenuous activity. It is an excellent self-interest activity.

    A. Passing
       1. Handling the Low Ball: A ball that is lower than the waist is one of the easiest to hit, but is also a frequent cause of the fouls of holding or carrying the ball. The best position for handling a low ball is to have the feet staggered, knees flexed, and arms flexed at the elbows and rotated so the thumbs are pointing outward, the palms up. When the fingers contact the ball, the entire body reacts in a lifting motion. The arms and hands swing upward in a scooping action. It is important that the fingers, not the palms, contact the ball, and that the ball is batted not thrown.

       2. Handling the High Ball: The chest pass is the most effective method of playing the ball. To receive the ball, the feet are staggered, knees are flexed, and the body is tilted forward. The elbows are raised sideward to a point in line with the shoulders. The wrists are extended in line with the forearm and the arms, wrists, and hands are rotated inward. To pass the ball, the hands are chest high, thumbs pointing inward. The fingers are flexed, forming a cup, allowing them to contact the ball. On contact with the ball, the wrists are snapped while the fingers and elbows are

pushed upward, sending the ball upward. A high ball is much easier to handle than a low one.

B. Serving
1. The Underhand Serve: Take a position behind the back line facing the net, left foot forward, holding the ball in the palm of the left hand. The left knee is flexed, the right knee is straight. Swing the right arm back and at the same time move the left hand (holding the ball) across the body in line with the right hip. Then swing the right arm forward hitting the ball off of the left hand with the palm of the right hand, raising the hips and arching the back in the same motion. Be certain to swing the right arm in a straight line, or the ball will be difficult to control.

2. Placement of the Serve: When the opposition is in formation, the server should try to place the ball in the right or left back area, and not near the net.

C. Setting It Up: A setup is a ball into the air near the net by one player, so a teammate may hit or "spike" it sharply downward into the opponent's court. The chest pass is the best pass to use. The ball is sent approximately ten feet into the air toward the spiker so it will descend from four to twenty inches from the net.

D. Spiking: The spike is a leap into the air and a sharp downward hitting of the ball into the opponent's court. A spiker must be able to spring easily from the floor, judge the movement of the ball, and strike it with a downward movement of his arm. To jump from the floor, step off with one foot and jump with the other. Stand with the right or left side to the net, facing the setup man. Much depends upon the setup man to place the ball in the proper position. The spiker jumps into the air and strikes the ball above its center so as to drive it downward. A snapping movement of the arm and wrist will drive the ball forward and downward with power and control. Aim for a weak spot in the opponent's defense.

E. Blocking: The block is a technique of defense used to prevent a spiker from driving the ball across the net. It is an attempt by one or more defensive players at the net to block a hard hit shot by using the force of the ball to send it immediately back into the opponent's court. An effective block is for forwards on the defensive team to spring into the air at the time of the spike, placing both hands and arms in the expected path of the ball. An effective block tends to upset the offense and presents another element for the spiker to worry about. To be effective, the blocker must anticipate the path of the ball and time his block with the spike.

DRILLS TO DEVELOP BASIC SKILLS

A. Passing
1. Divide the class into twenty-four-man groups. Have them form a circle and begin passing a ball around the circle trying to prevent it from touching the floor.

2. Divide each group with twelve men on a side facing the net. Form four ranks per side, with the first ranks passing the ball back and forth over the net until a pass is incomplete. Then have the second rank move up. Place the groups in a regular playing formation concentrating only on passing, using both the chest pass and the low pass.

B. Serving: Break the men into two groups—one line to act as servers, the other as retrievers. Change over frequently giving each man a chance. When the men can control the serve, have each server try to place the ball in the various areas of the court.

C. Spiking: Have two lines on one side of the court facing the net. One line is the spiking line, the other is the setup line. One man from each line moves up to the net at one time. The spiker tosses to the setup, the setup sets the ball up for spiker, and the spiker drives it over the net. Rotate the lines.

OFFENSIVE PLAY

A. Each member of a good offensive team should
   1. Be able to serve.
   2. Know the capabilities and weaknesses of each of his teammates.
   3. Have an understanding of all offensive plays.
   4. Be able to analyze the opponent's weaknesses.
   5. Always know what area of the court he is responsible for.
   6. Be ready to "back up" a teammate receiving the ball.

B. The big offensive power is the spiker. It is also necessary, however, to build a well-balanced team that can serve, pass, and "set up."

DEFENSIVE PLAY

The reception and handling of serves and spikes is the primary duty of the team on defense.

A. Receiving the Serve: The forwards move to the rear of their area. The left and right backs cover the rear, the center back plays slightly forward of the other two backs.

B. Blocking: The block is made by the center forward and either the right or left forward. The forward not executing the block must cover the position left vacant.

ABRIDGED RULES

A. The volleyball court is 30 feet wide by 60 feet long

B. The top of the net is 8 feet high.

C. A volleyball team consists of six players.

D. A match consists of the best two out of three games.

E. The first team scoring 15 points wins the game, provided that they have two points more than their opponents.

F. A deuce game is a game in which both teams score 14 points. The game is continued until one team obtains a 2-point advantage over the other

G. Only the serving team can score. If the serving team commits a fault, it loses the serve to the opposing team.

H. The team receiving the ball for service rotates one position in a clockwise direction.

I. The ball is put into play by serving from behind the back line.

J. A served ball touching the net results in the loss of the serve. At any other time during play, a ball touching the net is still in play.

K. The ball is out of play when it touches the ground or goes outside one of the boundary lines.

L. All line balls are good.

M. The players must hit or bat the ball; they may not throw, lift, or scoop it.

N. A player may not touch the ball with any part of the body below the knees.

O. A player may not play (touch) the ball twice in succession. In receiving a hard-driven spike, a defensive player may make several contacts with the ball even if they are not simultaneous. All such contacts, however, must constitute one continuous play, and all must be above the knees.

P. The ball may be touched no more than three times on one side of the net before being returned across the net to the opposing team.

Q. A player must not touch or reach across the net.

R. A player must not cross the line under the net; he may touch it, however.

S. For complete official volleyball rules, see the United States Volleyball Association: <u>Volleyball Official Guide</u>.